Science and Technology Acceptance and Transformation

Contribution to Public Health Quality Control by
the Pharmaceutical Industry in Occupied Japan, 1945–1952

SATO Akiko

DAIGAKU KYOIKU SHUPPAN

Abstract

This study aims to prove that Dr. W. Edwards Deming's introduction of statistical quality control (SQC) in occupied Japan significantly reduced tuberculosis (TB) mortality from 1950 to 1952 with the implementation of industry-academia-government collaboration by the Japanese medical products industry.

Based on its purpose, this dissertation asks the following research question: With SCAPIN-48 and SCAPIN-945, enacted by the Supreme Headquarters of the Allied Powers (GHQ/SCAP) in 1945, which called for the strengthening of public health, why did occupied Japan witness its greatest decline in TB mortality rate in the occupation in the period 1950-1952 rather than immediately after 1945? This dissertation also hypothesizes that the Japanese private pharmaceutical industry adopted Deming's SQC and therefore, through collaborations with universities, private organizations, and the government, increased its production quality and manufactured more diverse anti-TB drugs at lower cost in larger quantities.

At the center of this effort was Tanabe Seiyaku Kabushikigaisha (Tanabe Pharmaceutical Corporation Limited, hereafter "Tanabe Pharma"), a pharmaceutical company founded in the Edo period (1603-1868), which incorporated SQC into its anti-TB drug manufacturing process. This study focuses on Tanabe Pharma's QC activities under Deming's supervision.

This research also discusses how SQC helped produce better-quality drugs in large quantities at low cost in occupied Japan. Specifically, the anti-TB drugs domestically manufactured by the Japanese pharmaceutical industry improved public health by reducing the country's TB mortality rate, which for over 30 years had been the leading cause of death in Japan and the world. Concurrently, the increased volume, improved quality, and lower cost of the product helped Japan stimulate its exports. With the Dodge Line, which began in 1949, improving exports was imperative for Japan's reintegration into the international community.

When Japan surrendered in 1945, its public health program desperately needed improvement in all aspects including administration and organization, the health center system, specialized disease control programs, sanitation, laboratory work, port quarantine, education and personnel training, statistics, nutritional status, hospital and clinic systems, and pharmaceutical affairs. The TB mortality rate in the country reached 280 per 100,000, the highest rate in the world in the past 30 years (from 1914 to 1945). This led the Public Health and Welfare Section (PHW) of the GHQ/SCAP, led by its chief Crawford F. Sams, and many medical professionals, including researchers, physicians, and pharmaceutical companies, to work toward finding effective anti-TB drugs.

Deming was a professor of statistics at New York University and, at the time, a statistical advisor for the Budget Bureau of President Truman's Executive Office. On June 15, 1950, Deming, who was appointed by the Economic and Scientific Section (ESS) of the GHQ/SCAP, led by William F. Marquat, delivered a serial lecture on SQC. Deming also received an invitation from Kenichi Koyanagi, secretary general of the Union of Japanese Scientists and Engineers in Japan to conduct training for people in industry, government, and universities.

Tanabe Pharma adopted SQC in its pharmaceutical manufacturing process after attending Deming's lectures and instructions held in Japan in

1950 and significantly improved the quality of its anti-TB drug, NIPPAS. The name NIPPAS is derived from "anti-tuberculosis drug PAS manufactured in NIPPON (Japan in Japanese)". As a result, the Ministry of Health and Welfare (MHW) certified NIPPAS as Japan's first Quality Control Product (QCP). In the same year, following Tanabe Pharma's lead, other pharmaceutical companies such as Yasuhara Seiyaku, Sankyo Seiyaku, Daiichi Seiyaku, Hodogaya Seiyaku, Kuroda Seiyaku, and Shionogi Seiyaku, as well as the confectionery company Morinaga Seika, began mass-producing higher-quality anti-TB drugs, including para-aminosalicylic acid (PAS) and streptomycin.

In 1951, Tanabe Pharma and three other companies from different industries received the first Deming Prize, an award given by the Union of Japanese Scientists and Engineers to companies and individuals who have contributed to significant improvements in QC according to Deming's SQC method. Furthermore, in 1952, Tanabe Pharma was recognized by the Minister of Health and Welfare at the Tuberculosis Halving Ceremony for reducing the TB mortality rate by 50% from 1939.

The United States, which led the GHQ/SCAP, did not envision the Japanese as the target population that would benefit from the introduction of infectious disease control measures and the reduction of mortality rates. Instead, it prioritized American citizens who were GHQ/SCAP personnel stationed in occupied Japan and their families. Meanwhile, the Japanese pharmaceutical industry needed to address the high mortality rate of infectious diseases among Japanese citizens as well as the United States-led GHQ/SCAP personnel.

The United States sought to promote Japanese exports following the Dodge Line in February 1949 so that Japan could rejoin the international community. Japan then succeeded in exporting a larger quantity of better-quality products at lower prices because of specific procurement measures during the Korean War, which broke out on June 25, 1950, and ended in an armistice on July 27, 1953. Such demand elevated Japan as a supply base for the US military. As a result, the United States hastened its preparations against threats from the Union of Soviet Socialist Republics (USSR), the People's Republic of China, and other communist countries.

As recommended by the ESS, Japan's goal in promoting its exports was to reenter the international community following the United States's plan for reorganizing Japanese science and technology. The promotion of QC in industry allowed Japan to meet the expectations of the United States and become a supply base for the United States. However, with regard to public health in occupied Japan, the United States needed to strengthen its pharmaceutical industry to reduce the high mortality rate due to TB, which was called "the disease of exile." Despite the high incidence of TB, anti-TB drugs manufactured using SQC successfully lowered the mortality rates.

In conclusion, between 1950 and 1952, the Japanese pharmaceutical industry, along with universities, governments, and civilians, were engaged in a transformative collaboration fueled by adopting SQC principles, curbing the TB mortality rate, and safeguarding Japan's population. The acceptance of SQC addressed the health crisis and showcased the potential for industrywide collaboration to produce profound and life-saving outcomes.

Note

Parts of the statistical data and analysis presented in Chapter 3.1 were previously published in Sato (2014, 2016, 2021). This research revises and expands upon that analysis by examining the intentions of both the Japanese government and GHQ/SCAP support, as well as the activities of the U.S. Scientific Advisory Group, to provide a more comprehensive understanding of public health transformation in occupied Japan.

Contents

Abstract *1*

Chapter 1 Introduction *10*

    1.1 Purpose   *10*

    1.2 Significance of This Study   *10*

    1.3 Definitions   *12*

        1.3.1 What are "Science and Technology"?   *12*

        1.3.2 Four Actors: Industries, Universities, Governments, and Civilians   *13*

        1.3.3 Quality as Defined by Deming   *14*

        1.3.4 Deming's Statistical Quality Control in Occupied Japan   *14*

    1.4 Outline of Chapters   *14*

Chapter 2 Starting Point of Postwar History *17*

    2.1 Tuberculosis and Its Prevention   *17*

        2.1.1 Tuberculosis History in Japan before 1945 and Its Prevention   *17*

        2.1.2 Tuberculosis Prevention in Japan during World War II   *19*

    2.2 Reorganization of Science and Technology in Occupied Japan   *20*

        2.2.1 Changes in Occupation Policies   *20*

        2.2.2 The GHQ/SCAP's Approach to Japanese Science and Technology   *22*

        2.2.3 Renewal Committee for Science Organization   *23*

        2.2.4 Establishment of the Science Council of Japan   *25*

        2.2.5 Assistance from the United States National Academy of Sciences   *26*

2.3 State of Public Health Policy in Occupied Japan   27
    2.3.1 Notable Public Health Policies in Occupied Japan   27
    2.3.2 Administrative Structure Reform   29
    2.3.3 Health Insurance Systems in the United States and Japan   31
2.4 Acceptance of Science and Technology   32
    2.4.1 Deming's Statistical Quality Control in Occupied Japan   32
    2.4.2 Views of Statistical Quality Control Strategy Proponents   35
    2.4.3 Statistical Quality Control as a Catalyst for Economic Recovery   36

Chapter 3 Public Health in Occupied Japan   39

3.1 Transition of Mortality Rates in the Postwar Decade   39
3.2 Tuberculosis Control in Occupied Japan   43
    3.2.1 Tuberculosis in Japan   43
    3.2.2 BCG Dispute, the Immunization Act, and the Tuberculosis Control Act   46
    3.2.3 Ministry of Health and Welfare Measures for Tuberculosis Patients   47
3.3 The Public Health and Welfare Section's Emergency Support Measures   48
3.4 Intentions of the Economic and Scientific Section and the Public Health and Welfare Section   56
3.5 The U.S. Scientific Advisory Group   58

Chapter 4 Statistical Quality Control: Background and Necessity of Deming's Lecture   60

4.1 Quality Control before Deming's Arrival in Japan in 1950   60
4.2 Quality Control Requests by the GHQ/SCAP   61
4.3 Examination of Statistical Quality Control by the Union of Japanese Scientists and Engineers Since 1946   62

4.4 Deming's Visit to Japan   66
    4.4.1 Deming's Statistical Quality Control Seminars and Lectures in Occupied Japan   66
    4.4.2 Deming's Statistical Quality Control Lecture Schedule   68
    4.4.3 Deming's Quality Control Wheel Diagram   71

4.5 The Deming Prize   75
    4.5.1 Background of the Deming Prize and the Deming Application Prize   75
    4.5.2 First Deming Prize Award Ceremony   76
    4.5.3 The Union of Japanese Scientists and Engineers' Invitation to Deming after 1950   78

4.6 Quality Control and Achievement: Tanabe Pharma's Transformation   79

4.7 Deming's Paradigm: Consumer Satisfaction and Cost Reduction through Statistical Quality Control   82

Chapter 5 The Pharmaceutical Industry in Occupied Japan ······ 85

5.1 Evolution of Combination Therapy and Anti-TB Drug Manufacturing in Occupied Japan   85

5.2 Regulatory Changes and Healthcare Expansion in Occupied Japan   86

5.3 Transformative Impact of Statistical Quality Control on Private Sector Pharmaceutical Supply: Quality, Quantity, and Financial Growth   88

5.4 Comparative Anti-TB Drug Strategies: Japan and the United States in the Mid-twentieth Century   91
    5.4.1 Streptomycin Production   91
    5.4.2 Para-aminosalicylic Acid Production   92
    5.4.3 Combination Therapy with Streptomycin and Para-aminosalicylic Acid   93

5.5 Innovations and Challenges of the Pharmaceutical Industry in Occupied Japan 96

Chapter 6 Conclusion ··· 98

Acknowledgments ·· *101*
References ··· *102*
Appendix A··· *119*
Appendix B··· *121*
Appendix C··· *124*

Chapter 1 Introduction

1.1 Purpose

This research demonstrates how the introduction of statistical quality control (SQC) methods by W. Edwards Deming in occupied Japan mainly helped the Japanese pharmaceutical industry significantly reduce the country's tuberculosis (TB) mortality rate from 1950 to 1952. It aims to achieve this purpose based on the hypothesis that the Japanese pharmaceutical industry's efforts caused a higher percentage decline in Japan's TB mortality rate between 1950 and 1952 than at any other time in history. Leading such efforts was Tanabe Seiyaku Kabushikigaisha (Tanabe Pharmaceutical Corporation Limited, hereafter "Tanabe Pharma"), which implemented SQC methods in its anti-TB drug manufacturing process. This study focuses on Tanabe Pharma's QC activities supervised by Deming, who visited Japan as a sampling advisor to the Budget Bureau of the Executive Office of President Truman during the occupation.

1.2 Significance of This Study

History is "an unending dialogue between the past and present" (Carr, 2014, p. 28). In the United States, the SQC method was implemented for low-skilled workers in the production of precision weapons. In Japan, meanwhile, it was developed in a different field and supported by the government, industry, and academia. This research is relevant in that it links QC, which originated in the United States and was adopted by the Japanese pharmaceutical industry, to Japan's rehabilitation as an international community and the improvement of public health during the occupation. Specifically, SQC mainly helped the pharmaceutical industry reduce the TB mortality rate in Japan, which its citizens considered a disease that would ruin the nation.

This study highlights that not all Japanese companies thoroughly implemented the same SQC measures as instructed by Deming, who taught the basic concept of SQC at a seminar attended by many private companies from a range of industries. Even in the pharmaceutical industry, concrete production processes for each drug varied greatly. This study describes how the prominent Japanese pharmaceutical company Tanabe Pharma introduced Deming's SQC in its production process after learning the basics of the approach.

This analysis also aims to quantitatively observe and reveal that the Japanese pharmaceutical industry, having a history of more than 300 years, strengthened public health in occupied Japan and especially helped sharply decrease the country's TB mortality rate from 1950 to 1952.

This study investigates the relation between the domestic production of anti-TB drugs, the QC of anti-TB drugs manufactured by the pharmaceutical industry, and the TB mortality rate in Japan and presents evidentiary data. This study helps clarify the point of contact between the history of public health and QC. The succeeding chapters will focus on Tanabe Pharma, which substantially improved the QC of anti-TB drugs, para-aminosalicylic acid (PAS), and Deming, who taught Japanese companies his SQC method in detail.

This study builds upon and substantially expands previous research published by the author (Sato, 2014, 2016, 2021) regarding tuberculosis mortality rates in occupied Japan. While these earlier works established the statistical foundation for understanding the impact of quality control on public health outcomes, this research provides a more nuanced analysis by examining the complex interplay between Japanese governmental initiatives, GHQ/SCAP support mechanisms, and the strategic guidance of the U.S. Scientific Advisory Group. This broader analytical framework offers new insights into how various stakeholders collaborated to transform public health in occupied Japan.

1.3 Definitions

1.3.1 What are "Science and Technology"?

This study does not separate "science" from "technology" while referring to science and technology in occupied Japan. The GHQ/SCAP understood the need to reorganize "science" nationally in occupied Japan, describing it as an "influential social power" and recognizing that "science and technology" are defined as follows (Sugita & Sato, 2016, pp. 69-70):

(1) Strong "science and technology" are required to reconstruct the Japanese economy.

(2) "Science and technology" are the foundation of a healthy, modern society.

(3) Since "science and technology" have become an essential resource during wartime, Japanese people require the development and strengthening of a well-balanced regime of science and technology

with a sense of pride.

(4) Japanese people enforce the appropriate science and technology regime through the Japanese government system. Meanwhile, scientists should operate democratically in a science organization to realize such a regime (GHQ/SCAP, 1952, p. 27).

Therefore, ministries, except for Ministry of Education, assumed responsibility for science and technology, which had a direct link to societies of public health, industries, agriculture, mining, and others (GHQ/SCAP, 1952).

1.3.2 Four Actors: Industries, Universities, Governments, and Civilians

This study follows a science, technology, and society approach based on the view that science and technology do not constitute a theory but rather the social system. In such a social system, four actors have played critical roles in relation to each other: industries, universities, and governments, which are traditionally called the "technocracy," and civilians, who fall under "democracy." Although these two social categories have been considered to be in conflict, this dissertation adopts a general view of Japanese people's acceptance of the United States's science and technology from the perspective of "industries, universities, governments, and civilians" (Sugita & Sato, 2016, p. 70).

Furthermore, a deep understanding of this paper's theme would require a proper definition of SQC.

1.3.3 Quality as Defined by Deming

Before examining QC in occupied Japan and Deming's achievements and contributions, it is essential to understand how Deming defined "quality" and "quality control" (Deming, 1985, Box #124). According to Deming, "quality" is "the intent, fixed by management, which should aim at the consumer's needs." He considered that such intent could include plans, specifications, or tests that the management delivers to customers under its responsibi

1.3.4 Deming's Statistical Quality Control in Occupied Japan

Accordingly, when applying statistical methods, one must supervise "quality" and implement "quality control," which Deming called SQC (Deming, 1950b, pp. 4-6).

1.4 Outline of Chapters

The Introduction explains the purpose and significance of this paper and defines the four actors—governments, industries, universities, and civilians—as well as science and technology and Deming's concepts of quality and SQC.

Chapter 2 describes the history of public health-related QC during the occupation period. Specifically, it provides an overview of TB and its control measures in Japan before 1945 during World War II and the occupation. Next, this chapter discusses changes in the GHQ/SCAP's occupation policy, particularly in the United States. Afterward, it presents a summary of Japanese public health policy during the occupation. Finally, it explains the continuous history of SQC, in which the United States introduced science and technology to Japan.

Chapter 3 focuses on Japan's TB mortality rate, which had been the highest in the world, and outlines the measures taken by public actors, the Ministry of Health and Welfare (MHW), formerly the Ministry of Health, Labor, and Welfare), and the PHW.

Chapter 4 delves into the adoption of QC in Japan, tracing its evolution before and after Deming's arrival in 1950. It explores the roots of QC, including the GHQ/SCAP's role in SQC as well as the Union of Japanese Scientists and Engineers' (JUSE) analysis of it in 1946. Deming's pivotal visit to Japan is detailed, covering lectures, the influential quality control wheel diagram, and the inception of the Deming Prize. The chapter also examines the background and significance of the Deming Prize, recounting its inaugural ceremony. It also highlights the legacy of Tanabe Pharma and its attainment of the Deming Prize as well as comprehensively explores Japan's progress in embracing QC principles.

Chapter 5 investigates how the pharmaceutical industry evolved in occupied Japan, focusing on combination therapy and anti-TB drug production. Such development was influenced by regulatory changes and healthcare expansion. The introduction of SQC resulted in transformative outcomes in private sector pharmaceutical supply, which enhanced quality, quantity, and financial growth. A comparative study then contrasts the approaches by Japan and the U.S. to anti-TB drug strategies, encompassing streptomycin (SM) and PAS production along with combination therapy. Japan's pharmaceutical sector played a critical role in collaborating with universities, national and local governments, and citizens in lowering TB mortality, marked by innovative solutions in and challenges to the advancement of public health goals.

The final chapter concludes the dissertation by discussing the transformative influence of Japan's pharmaceutical industry in the adoption of SQC to mainly reduce TB mortality during the occupation. Collaborative partnerships involving the abovementioned four actors played a pivotal role in enhancing public health. SQC revolutionized postwar Japan and led to the mass production of high-quality pharmaceuticals, particularly anti-TB drugs. Tanabe Pharma's success exemplifies the impact of SQC on manufacturing quality, capacity, and cost. Comparative anti-TB strategies by Japan and the United States placed emphasis on diverse treatment approaches, which informed modern efforts. The collaborative endeavor demonstrated the potential of SQC and highlighted cooperation among industries, universities, national and local governments, and civilians in shaping a healthier nation and addressing infectious diseases historically and contemporarily.

Chapter 2 Starting Point of Postwar History

2.1 Tuberculosis and Its Prevention

2.1.1 Tuberculosis History in Japan before 1945 and Its Prevention

This section discusses TB, which was considered a deadly disease in Japan, and how Japanese society treated it. In 1945, the TB mortality rate in the country was 280.3 per 100,000 (GHQ/SCAP, 1952, p. 61a), the highest number of disease deaths in the world, which stood for 30 years until 1951 (Sams, 1949, p. 529). Even under such hopeless circumstances, healthcare experts worked hard to solve health problems in the country.

TB spread exponentially from the Meiji era to the early Showa era. In October 1872, the Meiji government, which realized the 1868 Meiji Restoration, opened a modern government-run silk mill with motive power in Tomioka, Gunma Prefecture, which was Japan's first venture into the Industrial Revolution. However, after Japan's disposal of government property to stimulate private industries in 1880, working conditions rapidly deteriorated. TB spread among heavy industry workers and soldiers, leading to an explosion in infections (Aoki, 2003, pp. 104 -110).

Prefectural TB mortality data in 1902 showed that Tokyo Prefecture had the highest rate at 337.5 per 100,000, which was 4.4 times that of Akita Prefecture at 76.2 per 100,000. In terms of TB mortality rates, the top three prefectures were Tokyo, Osaka at 319.6 per 100,000, and Kyoto at 312.4 per 100,000, all of which had large populations. Fukui Prefecture was fourth at 252.9 per 100,000, followed by Shiga Prefecture at 242.8 per 100,000. At that time, Fukui and Shiga Prefectures were home to many migrant workers in the spinning industry (Aoki, 2003, pp. 97-115).

The Japanese government had yet to promote substantive anti-TB measures besides those against bovine TB stipulated by the Cattle TB Control Law in 1901. With the development of the wartime regime, Japan's TB mortality rate increased, and many victims were young people between 15 and 29 years. The high TB mortality rate among young people in Japan severely influenced the psychological, social, economic, and political systems in Japanese society. Specifically, TB infections among military personnel and industrial workers were a serious problem that the Japanese government could not neglect as they were advancing various wartime policies. As a result, every year the government implemented measures one after another (Akiba et al., 2012, p. 52).

In 1934, Hokeneisei Chosakai (Public Health Services Association) of the Ministry of Home Affairs recommended that the government take the following actions to prevent TB: (1) add 3,000 beds for TB patients annually, (2) establish one health consulting center per 100,000 population and build 650 centers throughout Japan, (3) create facilities for TB prevention in schools for infant TB patients, (4) amend the TB Control Act to improve TB reporting, and (5) shoulder TB prevention costs (Koseisho, 1976, p. 329).

In 1938, the government founded the MHW. In 1939, the government established the Japan Anti-Tuberculosis Association according to the directive of Her Majesty the Empress to prevent TB and promote prevention measures with a donation of 500,000 yen (MHW, 1976, p. 329). In

1942, the cabinet approved Kekkakutaisakuyoko (Guideline of Anti-TB Measures) to promote anti-TB measures in Japan. According to this guideline, the government must enhance public health, create a sanatorium for TB patients, establish clinical TB, and strengthen the medical insurance system (Aoki, 2003, pp. 97-115).

2.1.2 Tuberculosis Prevention in Japan during World War II

In January 1944, the government reached a decision on the Kancho Kekkaku Yobo Taisaku (Government Office TB Prevention Measures) (MHW, 1976, p. 332). In November of that year, the government integrated the Koritsu Kenko Sodansho (Public Health Consultation Office), the Kanihoken Kenko Sodansho (Health Consultation Office), and the Shoni Kekkaku Yobosho (TB Prevention Center for Children) into the Hokenjo (Public Health Center). Operations began in 77 public health centers throughout Japan.

Before the government implemented the above measures, in March 1943, the Japan Society for the Promotion of Science (JSPS) announced that Bacillus Calmette-Guérin (BCG) vaccination was sufficient in preventing primary TB. The government had already vaccinated pupils who started working after graduating from elementary school in 1942. Based on the above announcement by JSPS, the government then increased the number of BCG vaccination target groups. This led to 10 million people receiving BCG vaccination annually since 1943. The Japan Anti-Tuberculosis Association built the BCG vaccination manufacturing site, with the National Treasury covering vaccination costs (MHW, 1976, p. 332).

Meanwhile, the United States was preparing its wartime occupation plan.

Documents by the State-War-Navy Coordinating Committee (SWNCC) described the U.S. government's postwar plan for Japan (SWNCC, 1945). The United States Initial Post-Surrender Policy for Japan (SWNCC150/4) sought to eliminate obstacles and alleviate social unrest in the military. As Akiko Sugiyama pointed out, the United States considered that military officers and their family members needed healthcare treatment to perform their duties (Sugiyama, 1992, p. 143).

The military service personnel training document titled *Civil Affairs Handbook Japan, Section 13: Public Health and Sanitation* reported details about Japan's public health situation (The United States Army Service Forces: USASF, 1945, pp. 71-74) and showed that the United States had information on Japan's public health before the occupation. Specifically, the United States knew that the TB mortality rate in Japan had been the worst in the world for years. The United States then considered that Japan should address its TB mortality. As Sugiyama stated, the smooth implementation of public health policy depended on the measures of PHW which was separately founded in October 1945 in GHQ/SCAP and returned to the Medical Section(MS) of the United States Army in June 1951. (Sugiyama, 1992, p.147)

2.2 Reorganization of Science and Technology in Occupied Japan

This section will analyze studies on occupation policies.

2.2.1 Changes in Occupation Policies

In January 1943, during a meeting in Casablanca, French Morocco, President Franklin Roosevelt and Prime Minister Winston Churchill announced that the Allies, led by the United States and Britain, would fight the Axis Powers, led by Japan and Germany, until the latter's unconditional surrender (Irie, 1978, p. 152). Among the Allies, it was the United States that took a serious approach to planning for East Asia and the Pacific, formulating six occupation policy options ranging from destructive measures to active guidance under the emperor system (Iokibe, 1985b, pp. 52-62).

The occupation of Japan had four phases: demilitarization, democratic reforms, anticommunism and economic independence (Nishizaki, 2022, pp. 195-197). The outbreak of the Korean War in 1950 marked the beginning of Japan's return to Western society. In July 1950, the establishment of the National Police Reserve Corps initiated rearmament and the expulsion of public officials as measures against communism. (French, 2014, pp.122-127) Influential figures such as Joseph C. Grew, Henry L. Stimson and Hugh Borton from the pro-Japanese camp in the United States played a significant role in shaping occupation policy (Iokibe, 1985b, pp.194-204).

Influenced by George F. Kennan's policy against the Soviet Union in 1947, the United States shifted its occupation policy from demilitarization and democratization to economic reconstruction and anticommunism (Cohen, 1983, pp.294-299). The evolution of the occupation is viewed from a world system perspective, with the United States facing a dollar shortage because of its post-World War II hegemonic role. In contrast to Europe, where the United States established its influence through aid, Japan faced a financial crisis, leading to a policy shift toward rearmament and economic reconstruction (McCormick, 1992, pp. 133-159).

The Dodge Line, introduced in 1949, sought to strengthen Japan's capitalist economy, linking it to Asian economic reconstruction. George Kennan highlighted Japan's economic role in the US Asian policy, which helped Japan expand into Asia despite its past aggressions (Igarashi, 2005, pp. 145-146).

After World War II, the US aimed to establish a liberal, capitalist order in East Asia amid opposition from the Soviet Union and China. Thus, tensions arose in the Korean Peninsula, in Vietnam, and in the Taiwan Strait (Matsuda, 2008, pp. 128-129).

Prime Minister Shigeru Yoshida played a pivotal role during the occupation, implementing reforms to reconstruct the economy and restore sovereignty. He balanced conservative views with support for the "reverse course" and Article Nine, denouncing war (Dower, 1985, pp. 142-156). Japan was limited to self-defense forces under the new Peace Constitution as Yoshida refused a larger army to avoid contradicting Article Nine (Hadley & Sodei, 1985, p. 152).

Although studies on reforms in occupied Japan have focused on demilitarization and democratization, the following sections will overview the GHQ/SCAP's science and technology approach in occupied Japan among other points.

2.2.2 The GHQ/SCAP's Approach to Japanese Science and Technology

The GHQ/SCAP viewed science as a vital social force that was fundamental for Japan's economic recovery, especially after World War II. They emphasized two primary goals: demilitarization and the democratization of science and technology. Recognizing that the Ministry of Education predominated scientific endeavors, the GHQ/SCAP believed that this control needed to be updated, especially when other ministries, including those overseeing public health, industry, agriculture, and mining, could also play pivotal roles in science and technology (Nakayama, Goto, &

Yoshioka, 1995a, pp.132-139).

To bridge the communication gap and ensure robust idea exchange, the GHQ/SCAP supported the establishment of the Kagakushogai Renrakukai (Japanese Association for Science Liaison [JASL]), which aimed to link the GHQ/SCAP with Japanese scientists across various fields such as engineering, agriculture, fishery, and medicine. Through the JASL, the GHQ/SCAP sought to obtain feedback on the best organizational structures in Japanese science and technology (GHQ/SCAP, 1990, pp. 33-36).

Meanwhile, the Ministry of Education initiated discussions with existing organizations such as the Gakujutsukenkyu Kaigi (National Research Council [NRC]) and the Teikoku Gakushin (Imperial Academy) to restructure scientific administration in the nation. However, these efforts were met with criticism, notably from the JASL, which highlighted several areas of concern with the ministry's proposed reorganization plans (GHQ/SCAP, 1990, pp. 38-42).

In 1946, as the Imperial Academy made independent efforts to reorganize science by collaborating with the National Diet, the GHQ/SCAP expressed disapproval over such attempts, highlighting the need for any reorganizations in the field of science and technology in Japan to strictly adhere to the GHQ/SCAP's vision and policies (Nakayama, Goto, & Yoshioka, 1995a, pp. 132-135).

2.2.3 Renewal Committee for Science Organization

In a joint meeting on November 27, 1946, among officials of the GHQ/SCAP, the Ministry of Education, the NRC, the JSPS, the JASL, and the Imperial Academy, the GHQ/SCAP emphasized Japan's need for science and technology reorganization plans, which led to the establishment of the Nihon Gakujutsu Kaigi (Science Council of Japan [SCJ]) in January 1949 (GHQ/SCAP, 1990, pp. 46-49).

In December 1946, the JASL led a meeting with crucial science organizations and the Ministry of Education, which resulted in the formation of the Gakujutsutaisei Sasshin Iinkai (Renewal Committee for Science Organization), which represented all scientists and aimed to determine the best structure for science in Japan. The committee agreed on several points, including its aim, the inclusion of all learning fields, the relation between science and politics, the concurrent consideration of applied and fundamental research, its membership composition, the establishment of regional liaison committees, and its association with the Japanese government (Nakayama, Goto, & Yoshioka, 1995a, pp. 136-138).

Subsequently, the committee designated seven primary learning fields with an eighth section called *Sogo Bunya* (general science field) which employed representatives from six organizations including the Teikoku Hatsumei Kyokai (Imperial Invention Association), Minshushugi Kagakusha Kyokai (Democratic Scientists' Association), Minshushugi Gijutsusha Kyokai (Democratic Technologists' Association), Kagakushi Gakkai (History of Science Society), Nihon Kagakugijutsu Renmei (JUSE), and Hokkaido Sogo Gijutsu Renmei (Hokkaido General Technologists Association). Among these organizations, the JUSE played a significant role in introducing and disseminating SQC (GHQ/SCAP, 1990, pp. 52-56).

The Keizai Fukko Kaigi (Economic Recovery Council), which was sponsored by private companies, had attempted to rehabilitate science and technology business fields, but the GHQ/SCAP advised that such reorganization be done with other Japanese organizations, which led the council to disband (GHQ/SCAP, 1990, pp. 52-56).

The Renewal Committee for Science Organization was recognized internationally during its inauguration ceremony on August 25, 1947. In early 1948, they presented a temporary plan to the GHQ/SCAP, which was not approved. They then presented a revised plan in March 1948 and submitted it to the prime minister the following month. One of their proposals was the establishment of the Nihon Gakujutsu Kaigi (Science Council of Japan) as Japan's top scientific organization and regional body for localized functions. The committee also made several recommendations on government coordination, ministry bureaus, and science-related administrative agencies. Before the appointment of its chairman, the reform committee set up an initiative preparation committee to execute the former's decisions (GHQ/SCAP, 1990, pp. 64-65).

2.2.4 Establishment of the Science Council of Japan

The Renewal Committee for Science Organization advocated the creation of the SCJ as the chief representative body for Japanese scientists, which would operate under the prime minister using state funding. Tasked with addressing significant scientific challenges, implementing its decisions, and enhancing research, the SCJ would also serve as the government's main advisory body on science with recommending authority (Nakayama, Goto, & Yoshioka, 1995a, p. 139).

With 210 members selected via a national vote of qualified scientists, the SCJ would inherit the functions of the NRC and feature the National Academy symbolically. In June 1948, a bill to establish the SCJ was introduced to the Diet and was ratified by both houses in July. Despite the Japan Academy's initial resistance to the SCJ's voting process, the GHQ/SCAP emphasized its democratic foundation. In December 1948, the SCJ's first election witnessed diverse representation, including a significant communist presence (GHQ/SCAP, 1990, pp. 68-74).

In January 1949, the previously deferred Kagakugijutsu Gyosei Kyogikai (Scientific and Technical Administration Commission [STAC]) was established within the prime minister's office. The SCJ Law outlined its advisory roles, and while the STAC functioned as a bridge between the SCJ and the government, its effectiveness needed further enhancement (GHQ/SCAP, 1990, p. 74).

2.2.5 Assistance from the United States National Academy of Sciences

In 1948, the GHQ/SCAP invited the United States National Academy of Sciences (NAS), which aimed to enhance international collaborations among Japanese scientists, for a mission in Japan to reorganize its scientific efforts and evaluate its science and technology initiatives. During this three-week visit, the mission noted Japan's demilitarized science and its positive relation with the GHQ/SCAP. They recommended strategies for training future scientific leaders, funding exceptional students for overseas study, promoting exchange programs, allocating funds for research infrastructure, and motivating scientists to strengthen various fields. By the end of the occupation, most of these recommendations had been implemented. Additionally, the Ministry of Commerce and Industry managed technical laboratories to boost industry and trade through research and development, emphasizing product testing and setting standards. All such efforts sought to improve QC in science and technology as well as public health throughout Japan with an emphasis on TB mortality rate reduction.

2.3 State of Public Health Policy in Occupied Japan

This section investigates Japan's public health policy.

2.3.1 Notable Public Health Policies in Occupied Japan

The GHQ/SCAP's SCAPIN-48 memorandum, established on September 22, 1945, and conveyed to the Japanese government via the Central Liaison Office in Tokyo, focused on essential public health measures for Japan's recovery. It provided immediate directives, including an MHW survey to assess disease prevalence, available medical personnel, hospital facilities, and the adequacy of relevant laws. Measures included weekly reports on infectious diseases, disease control procedures, and the restoration of civilian water and waste systems. The memorandum emphasized the reopening or maintenance of medical facilities for citizens, the distribution of medical supplies through Japanese channels, and the establishment of port quarantine control in coordination with the U.S. Naval Forces. It also highlighted the revival of civilian laboratories for public health work and allowed for faster vital statistics reporting. The document underscored the importance of controlling venereal diseases among indigenous Japanese personnel. Signed by Lt. Col. Harold Fair of the AGD, SCAPIN-48 outlined a comprehensive plan for postwar public health recovery as well as collaborative efforts between the GHQ/SCAP and the Japanese government (GHQ/SCAP, 1945).

The GHQ/SCAP also implemented various PHW reforms, which included the restructuring of medical education, the implementation of measures in preventive medicine such as public health centers and vaccination laws, and the modernization and democratization of hospital management, nursing systems, and the Japanese Red Cross Society. The GHQ/SCAP's policies sought to achieve "indiscriminate equality" in PHW services throughout occupied Japan (Sams, 2007, pp. 294-309).

The GHQ/SCAP's public health policy during the occupation initially helped implement the occupation policy, but it evolved to promote the primary goal stipulated in the Purpose of the Charter of the United Nations, which emphasized international cooperation and respect for human rights. This historical context is crucial for understanding the policy's evaluation and impact on Japan's history, especially during the Cold War (Sugiyama b, 1996, p. 5). Healthcare reform in occupied Japan, with its close ties to political and social policies, highlights the occupation period as a significant turning point in Japanese history. Postwar healthcare policy in Japan was influenced by Article 25 of the constitution, which guarantees the right to life (Sugiyama, 1995, pp. 9-152). The PHW implemented various public health policies including immunization; the revision of the Tuberculosis Prevention Act; nutrition improvement; public health center system reform; improvement of statistics on epidemic diseases, mortality, and childbirth; hospital reform; improvement of education of doctors, nurses, and midwives and their national examination system; Red Cross reform; technical guidance on pharmaceutical products manufacturing; and improvements in drug testing. The PHW's policies aimed to establish a sound system of improving, promoting, and managing public health activities and healthcare in Japan. However, their priority was the health of military personnel, which the GHQ/SCAP also reflected in their policy. Nevertheless, the intention was to mitigate social unrest among Japanese people by improving sanitary conditions and create situations that would help the GHQ/SCAP obtain cooperation from Japanese people more easily (Mizoguchi, 1995a, p. 252).

Before the end of World War II in 1943, Japanese scholar Hirohisa Munakata started conducting research on penicillin. Soon after the war, the Japanese pharmaceutical industry began developing the country's domestic penicillin production, which prepared Japan develop production of other pharmaceutical products. However, the domestic production of SM as an anti-TB drug began in 1950. In addition, the manufacturing of Japanese pharmaceutical products to address special procurement demands due to the Korean War increased by only 3% in volume. Therefore, the influence of such demand for pharmaceutical products during the Korean War was insignificant (Mizoguchi, 1995b, pp. 373-380).

2.3.2 Administrative Structure Reform

The GHQ/SCAP issued a memorandum to the Japanese government dated May 11, 1946, regarding the revision of the insurance and welfare organizational structure and instructed the government to implement health administration structure reform. The Japanese government needed to immediately revise the welfare administration system to perform its administrative functions so that it could respond to general health and public health emergencies. The government was instructed to establish (1) the Health Bureau, (2) the Medical Bureau, (3) the Disease Prevention Bureau, and (4) the Social Bureau and create local health and welfare departments. On November 5, 1946, the MHW revised the bureaucratic system by establishing the Bureau of Public Health, the Bureau of Medical Service, and the Bureau of Prevention. The Public Health Bureau would be in charge of establishing public health centers, promoting health and hygiene knowledge, discussing nutritional matters, and publishing public health statistics. The Medical Bureau had five divisions: the Medical Affairs Division, the Pharmaceutical Administration Division, the Pharmaceutical Division, the Hospital Division, and the Medical Treatment Division, which were added in February 1947, and the Maintenance Division, which was included in August 1947. The Prevention Bureau had three divisions: the Prevention Division, the Quarantine Division, and the Examination Division, which took charge of prevention tasks associated with TB, leprosy, trachoma, parasitic diseases, myopia, cancer, and mental illness. In December 1947, the Prevention Bureau added the Sanitary Facilities Division (Mizoguchi, 1995, pp. 257-258).

The formation of the abovementioned bureaus and divisions prioritized public health for the GHQ/SCAP rather than for the Japanese. Meanwhile, for the MHW, a Japanese administrative agency, the November 1946 appointment of medical school-educated technical officers as directors of the Medical Bureau, the Preventive Bureau, and the Public Health Bureau was a scheme to introduce medical science and technology to the administration (Amakawa & Sugiyama, 1996, p. 5).

The GHQ/SCAP initiated significant healthcare and welfare reforms during the occupation, covering the restructuring of medical education, preventive medicine measures such as public health centers and vaccination laws, and the modernization of medical systems including hospital management, nursing, and the Japanese Red Cross Society. These changes marked an innovative departure from Japanese healthcare history, which had spanned more than a millennium since the Taihoritsuryo in 701. The reforms aimed to democratize and demilitarize healthcare after World War II, granting people the right to life and equal access to high-quality medical treatment per Article 25 of Japan's Constitution (Takemae, 1986, pp. 432-434).

The GHQ/SCAP's efforts included the investigation of prewar administrative and health policies and the use of existing structures and resources to promote reform. This section also highlights private sector activities such as the pharmaceutical industry's domestic production of medications, including penicillin and SM, with GHQ/SCAP support (Mizoguchi, 1995b, p. 380).

This study discusses private sector innovations such as PAS and antibiotics and mainly focuses on Japanese pharmaceutical company Tanabe Pharma's efforts toward cost-effective and high-quality PAS production (Koseisho Imukyoku Kokuritsuryoyojokanai and Kokuritsuryoyojoshi Kenkyukai: MHW/Sanatoria, 1976, p. 161). This dissertation will explain how the private sector contributed to the TB mortality rate reduction from 1950 to 1952, attributing its success to Deming's SQC, which the pharmaceutical industry adopted during Japan's postwar reform era. This study also aims to analyze these activities by summarizing QC studies, including statistical methods.

2.3.3 Health Insurance Systems in the United States and Japan

In Japan, the Shakaihoken Chosakai (Social Insurance System Investigation Committee) reviewed the Beverage Report, which served as the basis for the postwar British social security system, and introduced this concept in October 1947. Subsequently, a US missionary group in Japan issued a recommendation regarding the social security system in July 1948, leading to the establishment of the *Shakai Hosho Seido ni Kansuru Kankoku (Recommendation on the Social Security System in Japan)* in

October 1950. Named "Recommendation 1950," it was considered the most reasonable policy during economic hardship due to the Dodge Line's tight money policy in 1949. This recommendation signaled Japan's first systematic demonstration of social security principles and systems, highlighting the right to live as stipulated in Article 25 of the constitution. The social security system, with its four pillars—social insurance, national aid, public health, and social welfare—has since been continuously improved to guarantee minimum living standards for the entire nation. The government was tasked with the ultimate responsibility to reach this goal (Sugita, 2008, pp. 46-49).

2.4 Acceptance of Science and Technology

This section adopts the view that actors in occupied Japan accepted the science and technology introduced by the GHQ/SCAP. It also examines the influence of the circumstances surrounding the actors during that period in Japan.

2.4.1 Deming's Statistical Quality Control in Occupied Japan

This section explores QC studies focusing on healthcare reform and economic reconstruction during the reorganization of science and technology in occupied Japan.

The GHQ/SCAP considered it important to introduce QC and management technology in occupied Japan to promote Japanese exports with good-quality products. On March 4, 1946, the GHQ/SCAP issued a "Memorandum on Export Procedure," after which Japan made its first official export trade after World War II. The Japanese government purchased export goods from Japanese exporters and sent them to a GHQ/SCAP-approved trade partner (Ichikawa, 1987a, p. 122).

By August 15, 1947, restricted private trades were allowed, which led to preliminary negotiations between Japanese exporters and buyers; however, the ultimate decision on transaction prices rested with foreign trade corporations. This system ceased by the end of 1949, but the GHQ/SCAP retained oversight. Despite advancements in industrial standardization and quality improvement led by the Economic and Scientific Section (ESS) of the GHQ/SCAP, Japanese manufacturers remained inactive, which resulted in subpar domestic and export-oriented industrial products in occupied Japan before the Korean War in June 1950. These products prevented Japan's international reintegration, emphasizing the need for industrial standardization, dissemination, and rigorous QC. In late 1949, as efforts to enhance the industrial management plan continued, the Scientific and Technical Division (ST) of the ESS aimed to engage management's interest in quality improvement through programs supported by the Gallioah Foundation and the ST's technology import plan for 1950 (Ichikawa, 1987a, pp. 122-130).

The GHQ/SCAP sought to overcome the low quality of industrial products. Initially, the focus was not on the improvement of productivity and modernization of facilities. Because the Korean War broke out and the U.S. military needed to procure various armaments in Japan, the ESS created the "Industrial Expansion Plan," which aimed to reconstruct Japanese industrial productivity. In the short term, the plan sought to facilitate the United States's procurement of military goods. In the long term, the plan aimed for an economic partnership between Japan and Southeast Asian countries. Additionally, the outbreak of the Korean War shifted the

GHQ/SCAP's interests in Japanese industrial products. Specifically, they intensified their demand for higher-quality Japanese industrial products (Ichikawa, 1987a, p. 130).

John W. O'Brien, the chief of the ST, warned after 1946 that Japanese products would not be able to compete with products of other countries without undergoing appropriate QC. Considering such warnings by the ESS, Japanese industries should have addressed the quality improvement of Japanese products more since they exported only to Asia, where high quality was not required around 1949. After the policy change in 1949 to designate Japan as the United States's industrial base in the Far East, ST staff, including Bowen C. Dees, who had a doctoral degree in physics, and W. K. Knight, who was a chemistry engineer, instructed Japanese industries to implement and execute QC (Nakayama, Takemae, Miwa, & Sasamoto, 2000, p. 12).

In Japan, technology-based associations, which included both public and private companies, expressed a strong interest in QC. The JUSE is one such example, which traced its roots to three Japanese technical associations: the Shadanhojin Koseikai, established in 1918; the Shadanhojin Nihon Kojin Kurabu (Japan Engineers Club), founded in 1920, later renamed the Nihon Gijutsu Kyokai (Japan Technical Association) in 1935; and the Zen-nihon Kagakugijutsu Todokai (All-Japan Federation of Science and Technology), established in 1940. Driven by their research and development of QC in science and technology, these organizations merged to establish the Dainippon Gijutsukai (Imperial Japan Technology Association) on November 3, 1944, which later became the JUSE on May 1, 1946. These Japanese organizations played a pivotal role in advancing technological QC, guided by university professors specializing in the field

(JUSE, 1997, pp. 1-5).

2.4.2 Views of Statistical Quality Control Strategy Proponents

The GHQ/SCAP stated that "[t]he desirability of SQC was, however, realized by GHQ/SCAP and a GHQ/SCAP expert was assigned in 1950 to advise the Japanese," and Deming was appointed as a statistics advisor of the Executive Office of President Truman (GHQ/SCAP, 1952, p. 112).

On March 8, 1950, Kenichi Koyanagi, senior managing director of the JUSE, asked Deming to write the forewords for *Hinshitsukanri (Quality Control)*, the JUSE's journal, to commemorate its publication. Later, the JUSE wrote to Deming requesting that he hold a serial lecture on SQC on April 1, 1950 (Koyanagi, 1997, p. 29).

The JUSE summarized Deming's eight-day lecture on essential SQC from July 10 to 17, 1950, by publishing a book titled *W. E. Demingu Hakushi Kogiroku (Statistical Control of Quality: Lecture Report of Dr. W. E. Deming)*, which achieved great success in terms of sales. Because of this, the JUSE invited Deming again from July to October 1951. Deming first delivered a lecture on QC to Japanese presidents and senior managing directors in private companies and then held a specialized seminar (Deming, 1952).

Meanwhile, American executives did not accept Deming's method, which Deming considered a bitter experience. Therefore, Deming strongly directed the JUSE staff to recommend SQC to the top management of Japanese companies.

In September 1951, the JUSE established the Deming Prize from book sale proceeds when the JUSE and Japanese QC experts held the first Quality Control Conference in Osaka. The JUSE awarded the Deming Prize to individuals who contributed to theory and enlightenment as well as to QC promotion activities and companies that changed their organization with a keen interest in implementing Deming's SQC (Nakayama, 1995b, pp. 271-272).

Motosaburo Masuyama was the recipient of the first Deming Prize (Deming Prize for Individuals). Other awardees included Tanabe Pharma from the pharmaceutical industry, Showa Denko Kabushikigaisha (Showa Denko KK) from the chemical industry, Yawata Seitetsu Kabushikigaisha (Yawata et al.), and Fuji Seitetsu Kabushikigaisha (Fuji et al.) from the iron and steel industry, which received the first Deming Application Prize, which externally promoted a company's corporate image and internally provided a goal for a worksite and became part of labor management. Each company then competed and made efforts to obtain the Deming Prize (JUSE, 1997, pp. 35-37), which significantly contributed to the QC improvement of Japanese products (Hein, 1993, pp. 109-110).

2.4.3 Statistical Quality Control as a Catalyst for Economic Recovery

Japanese industries welcomed Deming's QC method to achieve management rationalization without incurring costs. It was only when Deming came to Japan and delivered instructions on SQC that they needed more funds even if they wanted to import machinery, introduce foreign capital, and rationalize equipment. Because of SQC, these industries found a way to attain their goals. Deming's SQC became well-known in Japan earlier than in the United States, which had yet to comprehend its importance as most people in the country, including scholars, executives in private companies, and engineers, considered the concept of QC as conflictive with that of productivity and generally thought that they needed to sacrifice quality to improve productivity. Moreover, as mentioned in the introduction, people in the United States thought that the only purpose of Deming's SQC was to meet mass production requirements for high-precision weapons during World War II (Takeda, 2002, pp. 238-245).

Besides the United States's introduction of technology and capital to Japan, special procurement demands caused by the Korean War promoted American business management technology, which was supposed to be the best in the world at that time. As an authority on SQC, Deming offered helpful suggestions for improving quality and efficiency. However, without a stable export market, the Japanese industry had no opportunity to implement these recommendations. Nevertheless, orders for vehicles, ammunition, and electronic equipment necessitated by the Korean War gave Japanese industries the opportunities and capital to adopt the technology using SQC introduced by the United States, especially Deming, which guaranteed that Japanese industries would improve their productivity, quality, and efficiency. With these improvements, Japanese executives recognized that they could sustain the export market after the Korean War (Schaller, 2004, p. 99).

Deming's SQC lectures in Japan in 1950 were popular among the Japanese because there was little space for such audience in Tokyo, Nagoya, Osaka, and Fukuoka (Walton, 1987, pp. 20-25). With pessimism regarding the effects of the Dodge Line, midlevel Japanese scientists and engineers, struggling for an "edge" that would allow them to compete in global trade, invited Deming to conduct a seminar in Tokyo (Dower, 1999, p. 543).

Some scholars mentioned that Deming's QC method, which focused on a statistical approach, supported most of Japan's economic recovery after World War II. International circumstances after the Korean War led

Japan to export a larger volume of higher-quality products at lower costs. Although the ST understood the need for QC in Japan after 1946, it was only in 1950 that the ST persuaded Japanese industries to implement QC soon after Deming taught SQC theory to Japanese scholars, engineers, and corporate executives (Nakayama, 1995a, p. 271).

However, the high-speed economic growth due to SQC after 1950 had unresolved issues, such as "overbuilding, planned obsolescence, congestion, and growing stress of urban life." The Korean War simply promoted Japan's adoption of SQC for producing and exporting higher-quality products (Hein, 1993, pp. 99-122).

The above studies analyzed the economic context and historical background of Deming's SQC as it was proposed to the four actors in Japan—governments, industries, universities, and civilians—and explained the effectiveness of SQC. However, this dissertation asserts that each industry in these sectors integrated SQC into their management and production processes based on industry-specific needs. For instance, in 1950, many Japanese pharmaceutical companies attended Deming's lectures in Tokyo, Nagoya, Osaka, and Fukuoka. Specifically, Tanabe Pharma introduced SQC into the manufacturing process of its anti-TB drug PAS. The next chapter provides an overview of public health in occupied Japan, focusing on the need for the pharmaceutical industry to find optimal solutions to lower the country's high TB mortality rate.

Chapter 3 Public Health in Occupied Japan

This chapter examines the prevailing public health conditions during the occupation of Japan, aiming to clarify the initiatives spearheaded by Crawford F. Sams, chief of the PHW, to fix the severely affected public health landscape focusing on the pervasive threat of TB, which had elevated Japan as having the world's highest mortality rate due to the disease.

3.1 Transition of Mortality Rates in the Postwar Decade

As discussed in Chapter 2, which introduces relevant studies, postwar healthcare reforms became a case of the ideal implementation of human rights in the twentieth century (Takemae, 1986, pp. 432-434). The MHW prepared public health statistics to help manage mortality and birth rates (Sams, 1949, p. 529). These statistics showed that, until 1951, when the cause of mortality in Japan changed from TB to brain hemorrhage, nearly 16 years had passed since the principal cause of death changed from pneumonia or bronchitis to TB both in Japan and the world in 1935 (MHW, 1976, p. 39).

Table 1 presents the TB mortality rates in Japan and other countries from 1945 to 1955, highlighting 1950 as a turning point for the TB mortality rate in Japan. This is why the percentage of decline reached a high of 43.80% between 1950 and 1952, which was higher than those for other

Table 1 Transition of World TB Mortality Rates

(per 100,000 population)

	USA	Mexico	Hong Kong	Japan	Ryukyu Islands	Finland	Italy	England
1945	40.1	55.1		280.3		187	91	56
1946	36.4	55.2	109.5	261.2		178	84	53
1947	33.4	50.9	106.3	187.2		166.6	77.2	54.7
1948	30.2	47.9	108.9	179.9	65.7	155.5	61.5	50.6
1949	26.3	43.8	140.6	168.9	61	129.9	49.5	45.9
1950	22.5	41.1	145.9	146.4	66.3	93.6	42.6	36.3
1951	20.1	41.6	207.9	110.3	73	83.8	42.6	31.6
1952	15.8	36.2	168.1	82.2	78	57.7	27.7	24.1
1953	12.3	29.9	131.1	66.5	56.6	44.6	23.6	20.2
1954	10.2	27.1	121.6	62.4	48.7	40.4	23	17.8
1955	9.2	25.3	112.6	52.3	37.5	41.8	22.7	14.6
(1)	17.03%	13.22%	0.50%	31.10%	...	12.60%	26.70%	4.50%
(2)	29.00%	11.00%	15.20%	43.80%	(17.60%)	38.35%	34.97%	33.60%

(1) Percent decrease in mortality rates from 1946 to 1948, (2) percent decrease in mortality rates from 1950 to 1952.

Source: Kekkakuyobokai. (1993) *Kekkaku Tokei Soran: 1900-1992-nen. (Tuberculosis Statistics from 1900 to 1992)*. Tokyo:Kekkakuyobokai. pp. 64 - 65.
TB mortality rates for 1945 and 1946 in Japan are based on the following:
GHQ/SCAP. (1952). *History of the Nonmilitary Activities of the Occupation of Japan*, vol. 22. Tokyo: GHQ/SCAP. p.61a.
Note: The percent decline in the Japanese mortality rate, which is 43.80% from 1950 to 1952, is more significant than those for other countries or three-year periods (see (1) and (2)).

major TB-controlled countries. Other Asian regions such as Hong Kong and the Ryukyu Islands saw a lower percentage of decline for that period. Moreover, even compared with other three-year periods, such as 1946-1948, when the decline was most significant, the percentage of decrease from 1950 to 1952 was still higher (Kekkakuyobokai, 1993, pp. 64 -65).

Table 2 demonstrates how mortality rates due to TB and other diseases in Japan during the occupation changed from 1945 to 1952 and four years until 1956. It shows that the top cause of death changed from TB to brain hemorrhage in 1951.

Table 2 Mortality Rates due to TB and Other Diseases, 1945-1956

	TB	Brain hemorrhage	Diarrheal illness	Cancer	Pneumonia	Caducity
1945	280.3	...	...	...	...	...
1946	261.2	...	...	...	...	...
1947	186	129.4	129.9	67.9	130.1	101.1
1948	178.3	117.9	104.1	69.6	66.2	80.1
1949	168	122.6	87.5	71.8	68.7	80.9
1950	145.7	127.7	82.4	77.4	65.1	70.2
1951	110.3	125.1	97.6	78.4	59.8	70.7
1952	82.1	128.4	53	80.8	49.9	69.2
1953	66.4	133.7	46.1	82.2	53.6	77.5
1954	62.3	132.3	...	85.2	...	69.4
1955	52.2	...	...	...	...	...
1956	48.5	148.2	...	90.5	...	75.7

Source: TB mortality rates from 1945 to 1950 are based on the following source: Amakawa, A., Takemae, E., Ara, T., Nakamura, T., & Miwa, R. (1996). *GHQ nihon senryoshi, 1945-1951: Koshueisei (History of the Nonmilitary Activities of the Occupation of Japan, 1945-1951: Public Health)*. Sugiyama, A. (Trans.) Vol. 22. Tokyo: Nihon Tosho Senta. p.56.
TB mortality rates from 1951 to 1953 and non-TB mortality rates from 1945 to 1953 are based on the following source: MHW. (1955). *Isei Hachijunenshi (Eighty Years' History of the Medical System)*. Tokyo: Insatsukyoku Choyokai. pp.788-789.
Data from 1954 to 1956 are based on the following: MHW (1958) *Eisei Gyosei Taiyo (Summary of Public Health)*. Tokyo: Nihon Koshueisei Kyokai. p.55.
Blank [...] means no data.

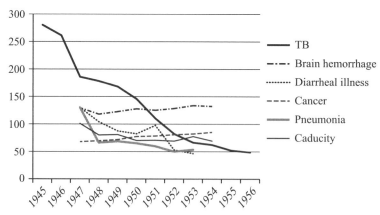

Figure 1 Mortality Rates due to TB and Other Diseases, 1945-1956
Source: same as Table 2

The highest reduction rate in TB mortality in occupied Japan, which was 43.8% from 1950 to 1952, can be attributed to the following reasons:
(1) To build nationwide public health centers (related to the public sector).
(2) To start the school lunch system (related to the public sector).
(3) To initiate the domestic production of anti-TB drugs (related to the private sector).

Regarding reason (1), the government enacted the Public Health Center Law in 1947 and accepted SCAPIN-48, which focused on the public health in Japan and established public health centers starting 1947. The reduction in the TB mortality rate can be linked to the period 1947-1949, which saw a rate decline of 9.7%, that is, from 187.2 to 168.9 per 100,000.

Considering reason (2), Japan started its nationwide school lunch system in February 1951 (Zenkoku Gakkokyushoku, 2019). Correspondingly, the TB mortality rate declined by 39.7% from 1951 to 1953.

With regard to reason (3), the domestic production of anti-TB drugs started in 1950, in which the percentage decline in TB mortality rate was 43.8%.

Considering the correlation between TB mortality rates and TB prevention efforts, the domestic production of anti-TB drugs led to the highest correlation percentage (Sato, 2021, pp. 58-59).

The facts above can be explained by Deming's SQC strategy, the pharmaceutical industry in Japan, and the PHW's public health policy. Therefore, the following sections will briefly discuss Deming's contributions, the pharmaceutical industry focusing on Tanabe Pharma, and the PHW's policy to improve public health in occupied Japan, primarily the reduction in the TB mortality rate.

3.2 Tuberculosis Control in Occupied Japan

3.2.1 Tuberculosis in Japan

TB prevention measures in Japan date from early times. In 1899, the first statistical study on TB in Japan was published, which showed that the TB mortality rate was higher in cities than in rural districts. In 1904, the Japanese government promulgated ordinances to prevent pulmonary TB (MHW, 1955, pp. 788-789). Ten years later, the government founded the first national sanitorium. From 1915 to 1920, Japan's average TB mortality rate reached 231 per 100,000. At that time, there was no effective medical treatment against TB, and the only prevention measure was to place patients in isolation. In 1919, the government enacted the Tuberculosis Control Law, but the number of TB patients continued to increase (MHW, 1955, p. 403).

The year 1934 saw the TB mortality rate in Japan at its peak; therefore, TB became Japan's most prevalent disease, leading the Ministry of Home Affairs to recommend strengthening TB prevention measures through the "Fundamental Measures for TB Prevention." In January 1938, the Fumimaro Konoe Administration established the MHW to relieve the Naimusho (Bureau of Home Affairs) of health matters (Aoki, 2008, pp. 667-670). Soon after World War II in 1945, the TB mortality rate reached an alarming 280 per 100,000 population (Sams, 1949, p. 529). The profound economic conditions, including severe shortages in food, fuel, and clothing, and the overcrowding and unsanitary conditions during the war resulted in an increase in the number of TB patients. In hospital facilities, however, the rise in TB patients was attributed to inadequate isolation, and caring for TB patients caused additional infections. Medical authorities considered these events shameful, but for the Japanese, TB was a disease to be concealed; as a result, public health officials could not easily find and examine statistics on TB patients (USAFS, 1945, p. 73).

In 1946, under the direction of the GHQ/SCAP, the MHW initiated a nationwide TB control program despite some delays due to other pressing epidemics such as typhus, dysentery, cholera, diphtheria, and smallpox. The program's initial phase focused on isolating active pulmonary TB patients discharged from hospitals, supplying necessary provisions, and shouldering 25%-50% of treatment costs. Prefectures established TB care committees to assist patients in sanatoria, support their families, and help them find work upon their return. Moreover, an intensive education campaign was launched, which provided medical and nursing experts with TB diagnosis and care knowledge. Media platforms such as the press, radio, posters, and journals placed emphasis on TB control both at home and in healthcare settings (GHQ/SCAP, 1995, pp. 52-54).

In the subsequent phase of its TB control program, the MHW expanded its efforts beyond hospitalized patients by recommending the identification and treatment of potential TB spreaders in the community. The MHW used the Mantoux test to conduct tuberculin testing for school pupils, factory workers, and other laborers. Adverse reactions led to the administration of the BCG vaccine, while positive ones prompted X-ray examinations. Active TB diagnoses were subjected to medical treatment. This approach effectively curtailed the infection chain, which extended to the wider community. These measures focused on resolving diagnostic and treatment challenges, lowering the TB mortality rate from 261.2 per 100,000 in 1946 to 186 per 100,000 in 1947. The implementation also helped identify more than 300,000 TB patients annually, with proper medical care preventing fatalities. Nonetheless, because of economic constraints, many unreported TB patients continued to require assistance to afford medical expenses (GHQ/SCAP, 1995, pp. 56-58).

In 1948, TB control officials in Japan integrated all phases of public health activities with welfare and social security, medical care, and preventive medicine, and TB control facilities such as health centers expanded their services and oversaw TB preventive education to control infections in the general public. Under the Yobosesshuho (Preventive Vaccination Law) enforced on June 30, 1948, annual BCG vaccinations were required for individuals aged 6 months to 30 years. From 1943 to the end of 1949, the total number of BCG-vaccinated individuals reached 31 million (Watanabe, 2009, pp. 37- 43).

In 1948, hospitals and sanatoria in Japan saw an average monthly bed occupancy of 25,000, which increased to 52,065 by the end of the year.

Influenced by a widespread educational program and the effectiveness of SM, Japanese people changed their attitudes toward hospitalization. In 1950, bed occupancy in national and prefectural sanatoria reached 94.5%. Active cases awaiting hospitalization in TB sanatoria were instructed by public health nurses regarding home isolation. With the increase in the volume of food rations for these patients and case reporting, as well as the acknowledgment of TB among the Japanese, medical experts were able to work on TB diagnoses. Mortality rates due to all forms of TB declined from 168 per 100,000 in 1949 to 145.7 per 100,000 in 1950, the lowest since 1900. Nevertheless, TB remained the primary cause of death in Japan (GHQ/SCAP, 1995, pp. 60-61).

3.2.2 BCG Dispute, the Immunization Act, and the Tuberculosis Control Act

In 1951, experts in Japan had the BCG Disputes, questioning the effectiveness of BCG. The Japanese government enacted the Immunization Act in 1946 and the Tuberculosis Control Act in 1951 (Watanabe, 2009, pp. 37- 43). The Immunization Act sought to maintain people's health by promptly responding to adverse effects from vaccinations and providing other necessary treatments "from the viewpoint of public health to prevent the outbreak and spread of infectious diseases." Meanwhile, the Tuberculosis Control Act aimed to prevent TB from causing personal and social harm and to promote public welfare by delivering appropriate healthcare treatment to TB patients. The Tuberculosis Control Act was integrated into the Infectious Disease Law in 2007 (Ministry of Justice, 2009).

Many events in history predicted the ongoing issues in health, medical care, and welfare, which required the acknowledgment process of the

Japanese alongside solutions. SM chemotherapy, which was imported to Japan from the United States in 1949, helped to considerably reduce the TB mortality rate in Japan. However, in 1951, there were delays in the establishment of the Tuberculosis Control Act. The government unified the Kenko no Ho (Family Register Act), established in 1871, and the Isei (Healthcare System), established in 1874, into the Naimu Hokokurei (Demographic Statistics) in 1886 (MHW, 1976, pp.171-174). In 1951, the TB death toll in Japan dropped below 100,000 for the first time since 1886, when demographic statistics were officially recorded. In 1939, that figure fell to nearly half the TB mortality rate, 212 per 100,000, when Her Majesty the Empress issued an order to prevent TB and to provide TB patients with adequate medical treatment. In May 1952, the government held the Commemoration Ceremony of Fifty Percent Reduction of TB Mortality Rate in Tokyo (MHW, 1976, p. 475).

Although the results of the TB survey after the ceremony showed a decline in the TB mortality rate, TB infections continued to widely spread in Japan. Since BCG neither prevented nor cured TB infections, experts in Japan disagreed on its effectiveness (Watanabe, 2009, pp. 13-14). Therefore, SM chemotherapy was adopted, which lowered the TB mortality rate and increased efficacy for affected patients.

3.2.3 Ministry of Health and Welfare Measures for Tuberculosis Patients

According to the National Health Insurance Drug Price Standard, SM must be intramuscularly injected into TB patients twice or thrice a week, from 0.75 to 1.0 grams (titer) per day. SM cost 350 yen per gram, which was expensive for patients (Pharmaceuticals and Medical Devices Agency, 2014). Its market size was 41,513,850 yen multiplied by its production volume in 1950 (Koseisho, 1950, p. 107). In 1952, its production volume fulfilled Japan's domestic demand and allowed for export. The MHW then stopped importing, improved the content quality of insurance benefits, and approved the use of SM among medical experts in September 1949 and PAS in July 1950. In April 1951, the MHW established the "guidelines of TB treatment in social insurance" (GHQ/SCAP, 1995, p. 211).

The MHW also announced its "Standards of Antibiotic Therapy in Social Insurance" in April 1953 and the "Treatment Guideline of Venereal Disease of Sailors" in June 1953, along with the full adoption of antibiotics such as chloromycetin and penicillin (MHW, 1976, pp. 456-463). Since Deming's arrival in 1950, the supply of high-quality medicines produced by the pharmaceutical industry in Japan has become stable (JSHP, 1995, p. 249). Cooperation between industries and civilians led to the creation of government standards and guidelines.

General Sams, the PHW's chief, who encouraged the domestic production of medicines in Japan, achieved his goal. In addition, the ESS was able to expand its mass production, export high-quality products, and lead Japan's reintegration into the international community.

3.3 The Public Health and Welfare Section's Emergency Support Measures

When the occupation began, the PHW implemented plans to prevent widespread disease among the Japanese, which were already prepared before the end of the war to protect GHQ/SCAP staff and their families, who were largely from the United States (The United States Army Service Forces, 1943, pp. 71-74). These plans, stipulated in the developed countries' military manuals and international treaties, focused on the health of people in occupied countries. These plans also described activities surrounding essential public health functions such as "the control, prevention, and treatment of diseases; the supervision and rehabilitation of hospitals; the furnishing of medical and sanitary supplies; the protection of food and water supplies; the disposal of sewage and waste; and the promulgation of such other medical and sanitation measures as would improve and preserve the state of public health of the Japanese population and protect the occupying forces" (GHQ/SCAP, 1990, p. 3).

The PHW arranged for emergency relief, including food, clothing, shelter, and medical aid, to satisfy minimum requirements, preserve the order of Japanese people, and allow them to engage in activities relating to agriculture, industry, commerce, and other peaceful matters. Local agencies were also established to manage emergency programs, and the GHQ/SCAP confirmed these policies. Furthermore, the Far East Commission formulated the above policies with various means of accomplishing their objectives. The United States government assigned Far East Committee members to the GHQ/SCAP, which had relative freedom in formulating public health programs. The United States supported the abovementioned responsibilities, and such activities eliminated any discrimination between military and ex-military personnel. The PHW's programs enhanced the essential occupation purpose to establish "a peaceful, stable, and democratic government that would support the ideals of individual worth and dignity reflected in the Charter of the United Nations." This concept was included in Article 24 of the Bill of Rights of the Constitution of Japan to provide a minimum standard of living for every citizen (GHQ, 1990, pp. 3-5).

Occupation forces started to examine the state of medical supplies immediately after their arrival. Pharmaceutical companies had available production capacity despite massive damage to their factories and were willing to begin production again. As a result, the PHW decided to (1) rehabilitate the medical supply industry and stimulate indigenous production rather than furnish necessary supplies via import expansion, (2) import only raw materials that were unavailable in Japan, and (3) reorganize the pharmaceutical system according to modern technology and professional lines. The PHW directed the government to provide medical, dental, veterinary, and sanitary equipment and products for appropriate medical care and treatment and permitted the use of the US Army supplies only when domestic resources were insufficient to prevent widespread disease and unrest among Japanese people. The MHW was responsible for developing medical supply procedures, and its officials underwent training to increase pharmaceutical production and establish an effective distribution system for pharmaceutical products (Kim, 2002, p.174).

Occupation forces confiscated all products and equipment owned by the Japanese army and navy (GHQ/SCAP, 1952, p.1). After completing their inventory, they returned non-war materials, including medical products, food, and clothes, to the Japanese government to be used by citizens. The government distributed medical products to physicians, dentists, veterinarians, pharmacists, and hospitals (GHQ/SCAP, 1952, p. 2). Delays in distribution were observed since most products had been stored in remote locations with complicated inventory, classification, and transportation. PHW officers directed the MHW and prefectural health and welfare agencies to conduct immediate distribution (Kim, 2002, pp.167-178).

The Japanese government's repatriation program required large quantities of drugs; vaccines; surgical dressings, instruments, and appliances;

hospital equipment; and clothing. The PHW directed the MHW to manage this program and shipped medical products to Formosa, French Indo-China, Manchuria, and the Netherland East Indies and other areas. For the program's success, the U.S. Army needed to replenish materials such as surgical dressings, instruments, sterilizers, syringes, and needles (GHQ/SCAP, 1990, pp.187-188).

At the beginning of the occupation in 1945, Japan's public health system desperately needed improvement in all aspects; as described by the CHS, "Japanese public health conditions showed every indication of becoming desperate" (GHQ/SCAO, 1952, p. 1). Specifically, the TB mortality rate peaked at 280.3 per 100,000 in 1945 (GHQ/SCAP, 1952, p. 61a), which necessitated an effective solution. Many medical staff, including doctors, researchers, and pharmaceutical companies, searched for an effective medicine against TB (Sugiyama, 1995, p. 5).

In 1949, a total of 600 kilograms of SM was imported using funds from the GARIOA and distributed to hospitals with qualified personnel and suitable facilities. This medicine was additionally supplied because the MHW and PHW permitted its domestic production (GHQ/SCAP, 1952, p. 60).

However, the MHW purchased SM by paying high royalties to Dr. Selman Abraham Waksman of Rutgers University in the United States. Therefore, Sams expected the Japanese pharmaceutical industry, which had been engaged in medicine production especially for TB, to produce them in Japan themselves (Sams, 1998, pp. 279-282).

TB had been "the leading cause of death in Japan since 1934." Annual mortality due to TB steadily increased from 1932 and reached a peak of 280 per 100,000 in 1945, which at that time was among the highest in the world for the last 30 years. Because TB was considered a shameful disease to be concealed whenever possible, only a few clinical cases were brought to the attention of medical authorities (Sams, 1949, p. 529).

The PHW started a TB control program and administered BCG to approximately 31,000,000 individuals by May 1949. This program reduced the mean annual mortality rate from 280 per 100,000 population in 1945 to 181.1 per 100,000 in 1948. Analysis of deaths by age group indicated that the entire reduction took place in age groups that were given BCG. Within these groups, mortality declined by 88% (Sams, 1949, p. 529). However, the mortality rate in nonimmunized groups did not drop significantly during this period, which was a lingering problem.

Sams, chief of the PHW, considered that BCG immunization programs would prevent cases of clinical TB. However, authorities still dealt with the problem of reducing deaths among the part of the population that had already developed clinical TB. Hence, a production program for SM was undertaken within the next two years. Sams expected that all patients would receive SM treatment (Sams, 1949, p. 530).

In May 1950, Tanabe Pharma was allowed to produce another anti-TB medicine called PAS, which was later called NIPPAS, in Japan (Oda & Matsumoto, 2001, pp. 161-166). PAS also helped lower the TB mortality rate along with SM (Sams, 1998, p. 286). Public health centers built in each prefecture by local governments responded to the needs of their residents. The improvement in public health in occupied Japan can be partly attributed to the organized efforts of public health centers established by local governments. In addition, budget constraints by the Dodge Line in 1949 stimulated innovations in the public health system such as the TB prevention program, which included BCG vaccination, the hospitalization of TB patients, and TB preventive education for residents from a public health system standpoint. However, because BCG did not work on TB-infected patients, it was not the final solution for reducing the TB mortality rate. Those infected with TB desperately needed anti-TB drugs to prevent death (Sugiyama, 1995, pp. 178-201).

The PHW made efforts to reduce the incidence of TB and venereal disease as both were severe impediments to the improvement of public health standards in occupied Japan. However, until 1950, TB had been the leading cause of mortality among Japanese people, which meant its prevention and treatment needed to be prioritized. Nevertheless, for PHW officials and Sams, protecting the health of American service members who consorted with Japanese prostitutes was more critical. Moreover, policies on TB and venereal disease were not clear until some years into the occupation mainly because acute infectious diseases such as smallpox, typhus, and cholera were more urgent threats to public health in occupied Japan. The PHW finally began addressing TB in 1947. These circumstances were found in statements that Sams provided to the Allied Council for Japan in 1947 (Aldous & Suzuki, 2012, p. 141). The PHW and MHW devoted more effort and resources to TB and venereal disease control through tuberculin, X-rays and blood tests, BCG immunization, and laboratory diagnostics. Health centers worked toward understanding the scale of problems and controlling them (Aldous & Suzuki, 2012, p. 141).

SM importation began in 1949, and chemotherapy of the drug helped reduce the TB mortality rate (Watanabe, 2009a, p. 13). Medical treatment using SM started in 1949, when 200 and 400 kilograms of the drug were first imported in March and the then in October. At that time, the volume of SM was only 1% of 60,000 kilograms, which the Japanese needed annually (Aldous & Suzuki, 2012, p. 151). Japan needed to manufacture anti-TB drugs domestically. The volume of more than 600 kilograms of SM was positioned for usage by Japanese physicians and to create demand for the drug in Japan. The GHQ/SCAP planned to create sufficient demand for SM in the country and wanted Japanese manufacturers to produce SM domestically and commercialize it in Japan.

At the Tanabe Pharma headquarters in Osaka City, after 1948, research staff began reading the latest American healthcare books in the GHQ/SCAP library, which was also located in Osaka. At that time, Ikuhisa Nakamura, a manager of Tanabe Pharma's Documents Department, found a paper titled "The Treatment of Tuberculosis in Sweden with Para-Aminosalicylic Acid (PAS): A Review" published in the pharmaceutical journal *The Lancet* by Swedish scholar Jorgen Lehmann in 1946. The chemical structure of PAS was similar to that of salicylic acid, which Tanabe Pharma had worked on for many years. Tanabe Pharma had imported salicylic acid from Germany since 1882 and sold the chemical as an antiseptic agent. Further, in 1897, Tanabe Pharma began manufacturing salicylic acid. Therefore, researchers and engineers were accustomed to devising synthesis methods and characteristics (Oda & Matsumoto, 2001, p. 162). Since August 1948, Tanabe Pharma has addressed the manufacturing of PAS under the supervision of Dr. Shigehiko Sugasawa of the Pharmaceutical Sciences, University of Tokyo. Tanabe Pharma successfully synthesized 500 grams of the PAS prototype (Tanabe Seiyaku, 1983, pp. 193-195). Whereas SM was a case of an anti-TB drug managed by the PHW, PAS was a case of an anti-TB drug that was developed independently by Tanabe Pharma, which also received permission from the MHW for the paid distribution of clinical trials to doctors in 1949 (Oda & Matsumoto, 2001, p. 164). Tanabe Pharma started selling PAS with permission to manufacture the drug by itself in

May 1950. By the end of 1950, a total of 24 pharmaceutical companies had participated in PAS production in Japan (GHQ/SCAP, 1995, pp. 211-212).

Penicillin and SM were manufactured with protection, technical guidance, and assistance from the GHQ/SCAP. However, PAS was considerably different in that its technology was introduced confidentially (Nihon Yakushi Gakkai: JSHP, 1995, p. 183). The high reduction in TB mortality rate started in 1950 before the Tuberculosis Control Act was enacted. As discussed previously, BCG vaccination did not help lower the TB mortality rate; hence, the outcome of chemotherapy at that time could not be ignored. PAS was commercialized and released two months earlier than SM. Approval for the domestic manufacturing of PAS was given in May 1950, while that for SM was provided in July 1950. Private companies received a corporate tax exemption for three years after completing new facilities for manufacturing SM. They also promoted their SM manufacturing projects. In addition, the government purchased manufactured SM from July 18, 1950, to the end of 1951 (Meiji Seika, 1987, p. 77). Manufactured SM in 1950 reached a total volume of 118,600 kilograms. Meanwhile, the total volume of manufactured PAS increased from 565 kilograms in January 1950 to 141,232 kilograms in 1950 (GHQ/SCAP, 1995, pp. 210-212).

In November 1948, about a year before the introduction of SM to Japan in 1949, a biological drug caused accidental deaths. In Kyoto Prefecture, 606 out of 7,642 vaccinated individuals suffered from toxic poisoning, and 68 died after being vaccinated for diphtheria. In Shimane Prefecture, 15 out of 322 vaccinated people died. In the Conference of Inspectors of Biological Preparations on December 6, 1948, Sams strongly demanded solutions to pharmaceutical quality issues. He warned that accidental deaths involving children as a result of cheap and poor-quality products manufactured by Japanese companies were disgraceful for Japanese society. This was because the Preventive Vaccination Law in Japan was a unique law that had not been established anywhere in the world. He insisted on the importance of controlling the quality of pharmaceutical products. In 1948, the PHW started requiring the pharmaceutical industry to implement QC (Watanabe, 2009, p. 84). Sams was particularly aware of the importance of QC and wanted the Japanese pharmaceutical industry to be independent by establishing high-quality standards and producing appropriate quantities of imported products (Sams & Zakarian, 1998, p. 139).

3.4 Intentions of the Economic and Scientific Section and the Public Health and Welfare Section

The GHQ/SCAP considered that Japan needed to rejoin the international society by rebuilding its science and technology, which is "fundamental to a sound modern economy" in the country (Takemae, Nakamura, & Amakawa, 1996, p. 27). The ESS, led by Marquat, understood that science and technology were the driving force for Japan's economic reconstruction after World War II. The ESS followed the U.S. government's policy, namely, the Dodge Line, to transform Japan from a defeated country into an economic power and supply base in East Asia (Takemae, Nakamura, & Amakawa, 1996, pp. 72-73). The ESS staff pointed out that the Japanese production process in the manufacturing industry, including the pharmaceutical industry, did not adopt any efficient QC system (Takemae, Nakamura, Amakawa, Ara, & Sanwa, 2000, p. 12). The ESS and scientists of the JUSE contacted Deming to deliver SQC seminars to the Japanese (Deming, 1987a; Box #15).

Sams expected to rebuild Japan's pharmaceutical industry and considered that only appropriate medical experts, good-quality pharmaceutical products by the pharmaceutical industry, or modern medical equipment and products could advance health and disease prevention in occupied Japan, which was underdeveloped at that time (Sams, 1998, p. 279).

Sams noted that the prewar Japanese pharmaceutical industry had been developed enough to widely export pharmaceutical products to Southeast Asia. Nevertheless, at the start of the occupation, he discovered a drug stock of poor quality. Therefore, Sams strongly believed that Japan desperately needed appropriate QC because the Japanese pharmaceutical industry seemed to place emphasis on the quantity rather than the quality of products at that time (Sams, 1998, pp. 279-282).

In August 1946, the ESS established the Economic Stabilization Agency (The Yoshida Cabinet, 1956). Under the supervision of the PHW, the Pharmaceuticals and Chemicals Safety Division of the MHW supplied raw materials or medical products. Even before the end of the occupation, all control on pharmaceutical products was removed, and commercial trades were organized (Sams, 1998, p. 281). In occupied Japan, the commercial development of the pharmaceutical industry in the private sector already began.

The PHW usually maintained contact with the ESS as stipulated by GHQ/SCAP General Order No. 7 (Takano, 2000, p. 163). From this fact, Sams, keenly aware of the necessity of QC, must have recognized that Japanese pharmaceutical companies participated in Deming's SQC lectures and trainings.

To improve public health and lower the mortality rate among the Japanese, high-quality pharmaceutical products, especially for TB, needed to be secured. Sams, who lamented, "The pharmaceutical industry in Japan rather focused on producing products in the view of quantity than quality," was aware of the importance of QC (Sams, 1998, p. 279).

The GHQ/SCAP aimed to rebuild Japan's science and technology for economic recovery, aligned with U.S. policy. The ESS, recognizing the vital role of science in post-World War II reconstruction, contacted Deming to hold QC seminars. Sams aimed to enhance pharmaceuticals through quality products and modern practices. The Economic Stabilization Agency, which was supervised by the PHW, facilitated postwar commercial pharmaceutical development.

3.5 The U.S. Scientific Advisory Group

The U.S. Scientific Advisory Group was pivotal in reshaping Japan's science and technology landscape after the war. Under the leadership of Robert P. Patterson in 1947, the group recognized the need to democratize scientific research and address product quality issues (Patterson, 1947, p. iii). The subsequent 1948 group sought to foster nonmilitarized science, facilitate communication between Japanese and international scientists, and support the Science Council of Japan in industries, agriculture, and public health (GHQ/SCAP, 1952, pp. 33-35).

The involvement of the NAS as a guidance and evaluation body was significant. Its mission in late 1948 observed the successful demilitarization of science in Japan, improved interactions between Japanese and foreign scientists, and advocated the advancement of scientific information exchange. The mission recommended advanced training, financial support for study abroad, international scientific exchange, and the establishment of research centers to further their aim. The sixth recommendation specifically encouraged Japanese scientists to contribute to science in industry, agriculture, and public health (Nakayama, 1995c, pp. 125-126).

By the end of the occupation, most recommendations had been realized except for the establishment of nationwide scientific research and education centers. Concurrently, the Ministry of Commerce and Industry operated technical laboratories to address trade and industry needs. The GHQ/SCAP recognized the importance of Japanese-led efforts in reorganizing science and technology (GHQ/SCAP, 1952, p. 78).

The GHQ/SCAP's approach, rooted in the belief that reorganization must be primarily driven by Japanese initiatives, was mirrored by the Scientific Advisory Group's stance. Their 1947 report served as a reference rather than a strict guideline, and the GHQ/SCAP's acceptance of the NAS report in 1948 further enhanced Japan's scientific international standing (GHQ/SCAP, 1952, p. 62).

Chapter 4 Statistical Quality Control: Background and Necessity of Deming's Lecture

In the 1980s, the West, which viewed the development of Japan's postwar science and technology as a miracle, tried to find the secret of such progress and stumbled upon QC (Nakayama, 1995b, p.269). However, QC was not a specialty of Japan despite leading the country into such a stage. This chapter will overview the QC methods developed in Japan.

4.1 Quality Control before Deming's Arrival in Japan in 1950

In the United States before World War II, mass production methods that used unskilled labor caused quality issues that were not prevalent in Europe. SQC, which emerged in response, involved sampling inspections to prevent the production of defective goods before final assessments. Additionally, the concept of Total Quality Control (TQC), which was initially employed by the U.S. military during the war, evolved into a method that viewed the entire corporate structure as a QC system. Rigorous QC, which included specialized statistical techniques, was vital in the wartime munitions industry (Goto, 1950, pp. 32-35).

In 1941, the Japanese Society of Mathematical Statistics was formed, in which researchers such as Toshio Kitagawa and Motosaburo Masuyama worked on the application of statistical principles to industries. Masuyama developed "estimation," a sampling method to improve SQC. However, in manufacturing, mastery of SQC took too much work. After World War II, in December 1945, the Japanese Standards Association was established to set and distribute standards. In August 1946, they released the publication *Kikaku to Hyojun (Standard and Standardization)*, later changed its name to *Hyojunka to Hinshitsukanri (Standardization and Quality Control)*. Furthermore, in May 1946, Kenichi Koyanagi and seven other engineers formed the JUSE to advance QC. Although the JUSE was initially significantly involved in a 1947 reconstruction conference, their attention gradually shifted to technological progress, drawing members from academia, government, and industry (Nakayama, Goto, & Yoshioka, 1995b, pp. 269-270).

With regard to knowledge transfer, a Bell Labs engineer working with occupation forces provided QC literature, which included Walter A. Shewhart's *Economic Control of Quality of Manufactured Product*. The Nikkei Group, in September 1949, became a pioneer in QC implementation to enhance productivity (Goto, 1950, pp. 32-33).

In May 1949, Eizaburo Nishibori and colleagues at the Japan Management Association commenced QC instruction to businesses (JUSE, 1997, p. 16). In September of that year, the Basic Course in Quality Control was established within the JUSE as a permanent offering.

4.2 Quality Control Requests by the GHQ/SCAP

The year 1946 witnessed the first attempt to introduce SQC. Upon their arrival, the U.S. military was troubled by frequent breakdowns in telephone communications. Keenly aware of the quality defects and variations in telecommunications equipment and facilities, the U.S. military recommended that the Japanese telecommunications industry adopt a new QC method and began to provide guidance. O'Brien, manager of the ST, in a *Nippon Times* article on December 29, 1946, warned that QC in Japan had a crucial role in winning trade competition worldwide. That is, if exports were to be delivered during peacetime, they would be competitive only if QC were in place. Before World War II, Japanese exports had been widely perceived in the West as cheap and of inferior quality (O'Brien, 1946, December 29, as cited in Nakayama, 1995b, p. 270).

Moreover, a corporate rationalization campaign led to the enactment of the Industrial Standardization Law in July 1949. However, in the period 1946-1949, the Japanese industry did not enthusiastically address this issue because its primary overseas market was Asia, where prewar exports had been strong, and according to the ST, "it was not so crucial that Japanese goods be recognized as having high quality" (Ichikawa, 1987b, p. 14).

During the latter half of the Japanese occupation, ST staff worked hard to implement QC for Japan's economic revival. For instance, in April 1950, the ESS invited American engineers to teach thermal management and open-hearth furnace operations at steel mills, which was a pioneering step in the complete introduction of QC methods (Nakayama, 1995b, p. 270).

4.3 Examination of Statistical Quality Control by the Union of Japanese Scientists and Engineers Since 1946

The JUSE, founded on May 1, 1946, succeeded the Dainippon Gijutsukai (Association of Imperial Japanese Engineering) and the Zaidanhojin Dainippon Gijutsukai Zaidan (Foundation for Association of Imperial Japanese Engineering). The Association of Imperial Japanese Engineering was formed through the merger of three major organizations: the Shadanhojin Koseikai (Incorporated Engineering Society); the Shadanhojin Nippon Kojinkurabu (Incorporated Japanese Engineers Club), which changed its name to the Nippon Gijutsu Kyokai (Japanese Technology Association); and the Shadanhojin Zen-nihon Kagakugijutsu Todokai (Incorporated All Japan Science and Technology Association). The Association of Imperial Japanese Engineering was established through the government's 1943 administrative simplification policy during the final phase of the Pacific War, whose goal was to unify engineers from the public and private sectors. A crucial meeting in November 1944 led to the creation of the Greater Japan Engineering Association, which dissolved after the war in April 1946, prompting the founding of the JUSE in May, with its first board meeting in July (JUSE, 1997, pp. 1-3).

In January 1949, the JUSE received a 100,000 yen commission from the Economic Stabilization Board (ESB) for overseas technology research. The reasons for the JUSE's acceptance of the funding were evident from its first meeting on July 15 of the same year:

(1) Establishment of courses for graduate school students

(2) Formation of research groups by core industry companies

(3) SQC research conducted by four individuals: Shigenori Baba, Shin Miura, Shigeru Mizuno, and Eizo Watanabe

Led by its chairman Ichiro Ishikawa, from January to March 1949, the JUSE conducted research to primarily address the third point above and submitted its first report to the ESB on April 30. The establishment of the Factory Management Committee in this research report became the motivation for the QC seminar and introductory course. This was the precursor and rationale for inviting Deming and building the project framework. From this period, the JUSE established the foundation for collaboration among the four actors: industries, universities, governments, and civilians (JUSE, 1997, pp. 13-15).

In March 1950, the JUSE published a journal titled *Quality Control*, and their general principles highlight the promotion of the statistical control method within Japanese industrial spheres. They also prioritized the creation of strategies consistent with Japan's industrial traits, contributions to the field via foundational research, and the dissemination of research findings globally. Additionally, the JUSE sought to support research groups on statistical methods, assist in theoretical and practical inquiries, and nurture relationships between engineers and researchers. With these principles in mind, the journal aspired to be the main resource in its field and uphold its foundational responsibilities (JUSE, 1950a, p. 1).

The journal's editorial direction covered a range of content such as essays, research, beginner's guides to SQC, detailed discussions on topics such as statistical mathematics and sampling inspection, local and international updates, literature overviews, responses to questions, and practical exercises and examples (JUSE, 1950b, p. 1).

Upon the journal's launch, JUSE president Ichiro Ishikawa mentioned in the preface that because of the war defeat, Japan needed to undertake major reforms in all areas in a shift toward democratic principles. Advancements in the industrial and economic fields are essential to construct national peace, culture, and democracy. Ishikawa emphasized that statistical and technical QC methods effectively reduce costs and improve quality—a philosophy that became the basis for QC discussions (JUSE,

1950a, p. 2).

Kenichi Koyanagi, the senior secretary general of the JUSE, declared that the best way to rationalize the industry and improve product quality is through SQC implementation and urged company executives to apply SQC thoroughly (JUSE, 1950h, pp. 6-11).

Eizaburo Nishibori, the JUSE's councilor, argued that future engineers must learn inferential statistics and highlighted the importance of understanding that quality is determined by consumer demand. He also stressed the difference between research experiments and factory experiments and emphasized the need for objective judgment in technology. In addition, he posed questions about the responsibility for defects and pointed out the importance of a quantitative analysis of product quality. He also asserted that if high-quality products can be produced, then all products can always be of high quality. He further argued that quality assurance efforts should always ensure consistency and that QC is essential in every industrial field (Nishibori, 1950, p. 12).

Genji Asada of the ESB mentioned that prewar Japanese export products had a reputation for being "cheap and poor" and revealed that from October to December 1949, the leading export complaint was poor quality, accounting for 40.9%. This was followed by content discrepancies (16.5%), shortages upon arrival (11.3%), incomplete shipments (8.7%), shipping delays (6.1%), and violations of importing country regulations (5.2%) (ESB, 1950). He highlighted the need for strict QC to enhance the international credibility of export products (Asada, 1950, pp. 46-48).

Hyoe Ouchi, a professor at Tokyo University and chairperson of the JUSE's Statistics Committee, discussed the application of statistics to industry and advocated for QC based on sampling theory (Ouchi, 1950, p.

3). Mitsuyoshi Inao, president of the Seisan Gijutsu Kyokai (Production Technology Association), asserted that factories should immediately implement QC and incorporate statistical methods because of the problematic situation of Japanese exports (Inao, 1950, p. 4).

Before Deming's SQC lectures in July 1950, preparations for the introduction of SQC had already been in place by March 1950 through collaborations among academia, industry, government, and the general public. Deming's visit was not accidental; it was the inevitable result of active research by Japanese scientists, engineers, and bureaucrats to examine the need for SQC before, during, and after World War II.

4.4 Deming's Visit to Japan

Following his visit to Japan in 1947 as a GHQ/SCAP statistical expert, Deming returned to Japan on June 15, 1950 (Sakamoto, 1950, p. 2). This section will discuss Deming's Japan visit from an invitation by the JUSE.

4.4.1 Deming's Statistical Quality Control Seminars and Lectures in Occupied Japan

After his GHQ/SCAP appointment, Deming was invited by the JUSE to teach a course on SQC. During his stay, which lasted about two months until August 22 1950, Deming held an eight-day lecture on "Statistical Control of Quality," from July 10 to 18 (with a break on July 16) at the Kanda Surugadai Auditorium of the Japan Medical Association and a one-day seminar in Hakone intended for executives (JUSE, 1950, p. 4). His simply yet profoundly communicated teachings left a deep impression on Japanese industrial leaders, technicians, and researchers (JUSE,

1950d, p. 1).

Despite the expectation that participants would have a university-level understanding of language and a foundation in mathematics, the course surprisingly attracted 230 participants from across the country, exceeding initial expectations. The content was based on American QC methods, including the *ASTM Quality Control Handbook*, and other QC fundamentals. The lectures were so well-received that Shin Miura, a permanent secretary of the SQC Research Group, translated the general theory of the lecture and introduced it in the JUSE's journals. Attendees were particularly impressed by Deming's clear and relatable explanations, supplemented by demonstrative tools (JUSE, 1997, p. 30).

The seminar's success was credited to Deming's expertise and to the dedicated efforts of several organizations and individuals, including the interpreter Hisamichi Kano and others who assisted in lecture explanations, technical support, and recording. The JUSE believed in the importance of preserving the contents of Deming's lectures. With his approval, they documented the lectures, which were later published in English and Japanese and distributed among members and the general public (JUSE, 1997, p. 31).

On August 19, 1950, an exclusive executive seminar was held at the Yama no Hotel in Hakone, which was attended by 48 executives from 46 companies and discussed the application of statistical methods to industries as its central theme. In its 50-Year Chronicle, the JUSE reported, "After the lecture, the executives unanimously expressed their admiration and commitment to implementing QC in their companies. Dr. Deming expressed his hope and belief that 1950 might mark the rebirth of Japanese industry, bringing prosperity and happiness to the nation" (JUSE, 1997, pp. 30-33).

In addition to these significant events, Deming held several other sessions in Japan that year, including a discussion with 27 company presidents at the Japan Industrial Club on July 13 (JUSE, 1950, August 4, Box #26) and an eight-day "Quality Control Seminar" at Kyushu University starting August 4 with 88 participants in total (Deming, 1950, August 4, Box #26). Throughout his visit, Deming's contributions had a significant effect on the Japanese industry.

4.4.2 Deming's Statistical Quality Control Lecture Schedule

The JUSE organized Deming's interactive lecture on SQC from July 10 to 18, 1950, with the following schedule:

Day 1: July 10
(1) Introduction
  (a) Explanation of the purpose of QC and its broader concept.
(2) Lecture 1: Controlled and uncontrolled variability
  (a) Explanation of controlled variability, uncontrolled variability, and the two types of errors.
  (b) Discussion of control charts to identify uncontrolled variability.

Day 2: July 11
  (c) Discussion on learning points through control charts.
  (d) Management of situations where the process is in control but does not meet specifications.
  (e) Exploring the advantages of being in control and determining control limits.
(3) Lecture 2: Some elementary ideas regarding the control chart
  (a) Preparing the control chart method for control condition

Chapter 4 Statistical Quality Control: Background and Necessity of Deming's Lecture

determination.
  (b) Developing the control chart method for maintaining control status.
  (c) Precautions for QC implementation.

(4) Lecture 3: Control chart method for judging whether control exists
  (a) Explanation of the relation between QC and inspection.
  (b) Description of different types of control charts and their construction methods.

Day 3: July 12

(5) Lecture 4: Some experiments with a controllable process
  (a) Case study 1: experiment involving the height of coking coal.

(6) Lecture 5: Control chart method of controlling quality during production
  (a) Discussion of the dual purpose of inspection.
  (b) Importance of maintaining quality records and various inspection data forms.
  (c) Examination of defect rates (p) and discussions on (p) control charts of ball defect rates in experiment 1.

Day 4: July 13
  (d) Setting control limits for the future.
  (e) Considerations when managing data represented in percentages in control charts.
  (f) Discussion of X-bar and R control charts and the use of control charts for chips in experiment 2.

Day 5: July 14
  (g) Analysis of points outside control limits.
  (h) Understanding rational data grouping.

(i) Discussion on the economic implications of control limits.

(j) Focus points when using defect rate control charts.

(k) Discussion of X-bar and R control charts, experiment 3, and chips.

Day 6: July 15

(l) Further exploration of X-bar and R control charts, experiment 4, and chips.

(m) Guidelines for applying control charts.

(n) Discuss defect counting (c) control charts.

(o) Progression of QC research.

Day 7: July 17

(7) Lecture 6: Acceptance sampling

(a) Introduction to the concept and purpose of acceptance sampling.

(b) Exploration of producer's risk and consumer's risk.

Day 8: July 18

(c) Explanation of OC curves and AOQ curves.

(d) Discussion on single-sampling inspection plans and associated risks.

(e) Introduction to double-sampling inspection plans.

(f) Important considerations for implementing sampling inspections.

Closing remarks of the lecture

Source: JUSE. (1997). *Soritsu Gojunenshi (50 -Year Chronicle)*. (p. 31) Tokyo: JUSE. The author translated the description from Japanese to English.

Deming devoted four days to lecture 5 and provided various examples of control charts as part of his SQC teachings. Control charts are graphical tools for monitoring and analyzing process variations. They help determine whether a process is stable (in control) or exhibiting special-cause variation (out of control). Deming's emphasis on control charts was a cornerstone of quality and process improvement. The following are some of the key control charts that Deming likely discussed in his lectures:

(1) X-bar and R control charts: The X-bar (average) and R (range). control charts monitor the central tendency and dispersion of a process. They help identify shifts or changes in the process mean or variability. The X-bar chart tracks the average of a sample, while the R control chart monitors the range between the highest and lowest values in the same sample (Koyanagi, 1950b, p. 20).

(2) (p) control chart: The (p) control chart tracks the proportion of defective items in a sample, which benefits processes with varying sample sizes. This chart helps identify shifts in defect rates over time (Koyanagi, 1950b, p. 23).

(3) (c) control chart: The (c) control chart monitors the number of defects per unit and is suitable for processes that inspect or produce a fixed number of items (Koyanagi, 1950b, p. 25).

These control charts help evaluate the stability of a process and identify potential critical issues. In his lectures, Deming likely explained how to construct these charts, interpret their patterns, and make informed decisions based on such information.

The above control charts are one aspect of Deming's comprehensive QC approach. His lectures focused on utilizing data and statistical methods to understand and manage processes, continuously improve quality, and reduce variation to achieve better results.

4.4.3 Deming's Quality Control Wheel Diagram

In an article published in the JUSE's journal Quality Control, Deming provided a comprehensive overview of the core contents of his eight-day lecture series. He emphasized that extensive and purposeful efforts in two primary areas are required for quality control to yield meaningful benefits. The first focuses on ensuring participants thoroughly understand proper Quality Control principles and their practical application in the workplace. This understanding is crucial for successfully integrating these principles into their daily operations.

The second key area Deming addressed was the recognition that the eight-day lecture format, while valuable, represented only an initial introduction to Quality Control concepts. He stressed that participants must acknowledge that mastering Quality Control required significantly more time and dedication than could be accommodated in the eight-day format. This realization was essential for setting appropriate expectations and commitment levels among trainees.

Deming was particularly clear about positioning the eight-day lecture as a starting point rather than a comprehensive course. To illustrate this concept, he employed a memorable metaphor, comparing Quality Control to a wheel divided into eight sections (Figure 2), each requiring assistance to turn properly (JUSE, 1950, p. 5).

This metaphor effectively communicated the interconnected nature of Quality Control components and the ongoing effort required to maintain them. Through this explanation, he emphasized that Quality Control was not a magical solution but a systematic approach requiring sustained dedication and persistence for successful implementation.

Deming elaborated on eight essential aspects of quality management that form a comprehensive framework. The first component focuses on quality consciousness, emphasizing the importance of a passionate commitment to producing goods that meet societal needs while maintaining

Chapter 4 Statistical Quality Control: Background and Necessity of Deming's Lecture 73

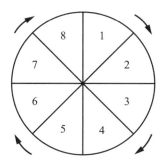

Figure 2 Wheel of Quality Control

Source: Deming, W.E. (1950). Tokeiteki Hinshitsukanri towa Nanika (What is Statistical Quality Control?). *Hinshitsukanri (Quality Control)*. Miura, S. (Trans.). Vol. 1 No. 6. Tokyo: JUSE. p. 5.

appropriate quality levels. Deming notably cautioned against excessive quality, arguing that products exceeding necessary quality standards become prohibitively expensive and potentially unmarketable.

The second aspect addresses quality responsibility, which encompasses accountability for the product and an organizational commitment to building public trust through consistent quality delivery. Research constitutes the third major component, which Deming broke down into several crucial areas: the economic evaluation and utilization of raw materials, locations, manufacturing equipment, and transportation methods; work efficiency analysis; machinery and equipment operation accuracy assessment; and research into worker training, education, and operational improvements.

The fourth element centers on product design, improvement, and establishment of quality standards, while the fifth component focuses on the manufacturing economy, with quality control serving as a primary tool for achieving economic efficiency. Product inspection forms the sixth component, involving a comprehensive evaluation process where staff members assess multiple factors: the product's quality level, its ability to meet buyer satisfaction, and its potential to generate repeat purchases rather than customers switching to alternative products.

The seventh component involves improvement initiatives based on inspection findings, requiring staff to evaluate and potentially modify design specifications, target quality levels, or manufacturing methodologies. The final component addresses sales channel expansion, which Deming identified as crucial for achieving manufacturing economies of scale. He emphasized that broader distribution networks contribute to more economical manufacturing processes, creating a virtuous cycle of quality and efficiency (Deming , 1950b, pp. 4-5).

The explanation discusses a continuous cycle of eight sections symbolizing an ongoing QC process. The emphasis is on avoiding shortcuts; staff should continually progress through these sections, starting over at the first after reaching the eighth. Manufacturers are advised to approach QC holistically across all sections, and not just focusing on the fifth relating to economics. An eight-day seminar is organized based on this philosophy (Deming, 1950b, p. 5).

Regarding sections 3 to 8 of the wheel, understanding statistical sampling, experimental design, and QC is essential. While specialization is possible, true expertise requires knowledge of all QC methods for creating attractive and cost-efficient products. Maintaining production vigilance to meet size, quality, and customer preferences is highlighted. Meeting technical standards is not enough; products must generate buyer satisfaction (Deming, 1950b, p. 5).

Neglecting areas outside one's expertise (e.g., focusing on section 5 but ignoring section 6 and beyond) can lead to business failure. Successful QC means adhering to the process rather than taking shortcuts. The importance of the first two points is emphasized, stemming from management's commitment to ensuring product quality, assuming responsibility, and building trust. Manufacturers should prioritize the confident production of reputable products for the long term (Deming, 1952, pp. 88-89).

Deming asserted that building, rebuilding, and stabilizing Japanese industry depends on comprehensive QC across all eight sections and insisted that solely focusing on the fifth section would result in useless products regardless of refinement or cost-effectiveness (Deming, 1950b, p. 5). Overall, Deming sought to install QC in its entirety in an organization during the eight-day lecture.

4.5 The Deming Prize

The JUSE's board of directors established the Deming Prize through a resolution to commemorate Deming's friendship and achievements with Japanese scientists, engineers, and other Japanese who visited Japan in 1950 (JUSE, 1997, p. 31).

4.5.1 Background of the Deming Prize and the Deming Application Prize

The Deming Prize Committee created the award to recognize Deming's contributions. Deming's lectures were compiled by the JUSE and titled "Dr. Deming's Lectures on Statistical Control of Quality." Deming donated the transcripts to the JUSE, inspiring the creation of the award, which aimed to honor Deming, promote QC in Japan, recognize contributions to QC research and education, and commend outstanding implementations of SQC. The committee had 25 members from various sectors (see Appendix

A) (JUSE, 1997, p. 34).

The "Regulations for the Call for Candidates for the First Deming Prize Award" outline the criteria for Deming Prize candidates, including those who have had a significant impact on QC through publications, achievements in implementation, education, and other accomplishments. Eligible parties include individuals, groups, companies, factories, academic associations, and organizations. Initially, the Deming Prize had two types: the Deming Prize and the Deming Application Prize. Eventually, the Deming Prize Committee would establish additional categories such as the Deming Application Prize for Small Companies, the Deming Application Prize for Divisions, and the Quality Control Award for Operations Business Units; however, it would later abolish some awards. Ultimately, the committee streamlined their selection process for the Deming Application Prize (JUSE, 1997, p. 34).

As of February 2023, there have been 85 individual recipients of the Deming Prize (called the Deming Prize for Individuals since 2012), including Motosaburo Masuyama, who was awarded in 1951. The Deming Distinguished Service Award for Dissemination and Promotion (Overseas) has been awarded to the following individuals or organizations: Gregory H. Watson (Finland) in 2009, Janak Mehta (India) in 2012, Kan Trakulhoon (Thailand) in 2014, Venu Srinivasan (India) in 2019 and L. Ganesh (India) in 2022 (JUSE, 2023).

4.5.2 First Deming Prize Award Ceremony

In 1951, the Osaka Chamber of Commerce and Industry hosted the first Deming Prize Award Ceremony and the QC convention. The event was attended by more than 500 individuals, including Deming himself.

During the ceremony, Deming presented certificates and awards to the winners and delivered a speech highlighting the importance of statistical techniques in manufacturing. The first recipients of the Deming Prize for Industrial Applications of Statistical Methods were University of Tokyo lecturer Motosaburo Masuyama, PhD, and companies Tanabe Pharma, Showa Denko KK, Yawata Steel Corporation, and Fuji Steel Corporation. The event also featured commemorative lectures and presentations by various dignitaries and prize winners. The Deming Prize Committee sponsored the Deming Prize, with support from the JUSE, the Agency of Industrial Science and Technology, and Nihon Keizai Shimbun Inc. The award symbolized collaborative efforts among governments, industries, universities, and civilians (JUSE, 1951, p. 6).

Before the first Deming Prize Award Ceremony, the JUSE established several committee rules. The chairman of the Deming Prize Committee was the president of the JUSE. Incoming committee secretaries were appointed annually after the Deming Prize presentation ceremony. The chairperson organized committee and executive committee meetings, and decisions were via majority vote (with the chairperson's decision as a tiebreaker), and meetings required a majority member attendance. The committee could form subcommittees for important issues, and academic experts could be temporary members. The committee enforced the rules, accepted nominations, conducted reviews, announced awardees, and oversaw examinations and investigations. It also determined the number and extent of awards, gave supplementary prizes, and maintained records. Travel expenses for inspections could be reimbursed mainly through the prize fund (see Appendix B) (JUSE, 1997, p. 37).

The Deming Prize Committee also provided some regulations. The

Deming Prize would commemorate Deming's guidance on industrial SQC. The committee would award the prize to those excelling in theory and application, those with outstanding achievements in SQC application, and those who have significantly contributed to its implementation. The Deming Prize Fund would consist mainly of royalties, donations, and contributions related to Deming's works. The prize would be awarded annually by the committee, chaired by the JUSE's president, who would appoint committee members. Deming Award Committee rules would be separate, and the JUSE's secretariat would administer and supervise the Deming Prize and Fund (see Appendix B) (JUSE, 1997, p. 37).

4.5.3 The Union of Japanese Scientists and Engineers' Invitation to Deming after 1950

In 1951, Deming returned to Japan upon JUSE's invitation, staying for 66 days from July 28 to October 1, during which he conducted various QC workshops. Notable sessions included management leader training, market research workshops, basic QC courses, and advanced QC training. Deming delivered lectures and provided exercises to industry professionals, educators, and organizations on topics such as statistical techniques, QC essentials, and advanced quality methodologies. He also held JUSE-sponsored workshops in different locations, addressing local governments, organizations, and educational institutions. Deming's visit covered lectures, meetings, and trips to notable companies and universities including Osaka University, Fuji Photo Film, Furukawa Electric, Asahi Kasei Kogyo, and Toyo Reiyon (JUSE, 1951, pp. 5-8).

In January 1952, Deming visited Japan again upon the JUSE's invitation after attending the Universal Statistical Congress in India. Before his return on January 15, he participated in three key events. First, he held a "Market Research Guidance Clinic," which offered guidance based on market research conducted by companies that participated in his 1951 course. Second, he taught the application of QC and new statistical methods in market research to 12 business leaders in a "Management Leaders' Seminar." Lastly, he delivered a public lecture titled "Quality Control and International Trade," which he cosponsored with the JUSE, the Tokyo Chamber of Commerce and Industry, and Nihon Keizai Shimbun. In this lecture, Deming highlighted the significance of using statistical techniques and QC as essential aspects of international trade (JUSE, 1997, p. 39).

Hiroshi Sugiyama, who interpreted for Deming's lectures at Kyushu University in 1950 and for several lectures in Japan after 1951, was awarded the doctor of medicine and doctor of science degrees and continued his research as a professor at Osaka University's Faculty of Engineering (Sugiyama, 1978, pp. 53-57).

4.6 Quality Control and Achievement: Tanabe Pharma's Transformation

Tanabe Pharma, which traces its lineage back to 1720, is a testament to enduring tradition and transformative evolution. Founded as Tanabe Gohei, a drug wholesaler, this company embraced change with the surge in Western medicine, transitioning into a pioneering pharmaceutical force by the mid-Meiji era. Its milestones included the construction of pharmaceutical factories in the cities of Osaka and Onoda, solidifying Tanabe Pharma's metamorphosis into a modern pharmaceutical company. Established as a limited liability company on December 13, 1933, Tanabe Pharma embarked on an unwavering journey marked by commitment and progress (Tanabe Seiyaku, 1983, p. 114).

Emerging from a disaster that befell the research institute in May 1945, Tanabe Pharma recognized its need for enhanced QC measures. Seizing the opportunity to systematize the company's manufacturing processes, Tanabe Pharma's president ardently pursued this aspiration. Frederick Winslow Taylor's scientific management method transformed factory work by applying objective analysis to increase labor efficiency. It aimed to reduce labor costs while raising wages. Taylor's approach, summarized as "Plan, do, and see," was based on meticulous observation of organizational behavior. Tanabe Pharma adopted this systematic approach, likely conducting detailed analyses of work processes. This allowed the company to identify inefficiencies, streamline operations, and make data-driven improvements. Guided by the Osaka Prefectural Industrial Efficiency Research Institute, this approach enabled Tanabe Pharma to continuously enhance productivity and adapt to market changes (JUSE, 1950d, pp. 7-11). Its turning point took place in 1947 with a pivotal visit from Ken Kayano, manager of the Telecommunications Research Institute of the Ministry of Telecommunications (established in 1948, later the Telegraph and Telephone Public Corporation in 1952 and the Nippon Telegraph and Telephone Corporation in 1985), who unveiled QC principles to company executives (JUSE, 1950d, pp. 7-11). This ignited research spearheaded by Matao Watanabe and Tadashi Asakura, which led to the foundation of Z1 QC practices at the production site (Demingusho Iinkai, 1950, p. 11). Z1 is a wartime standard in the United States (Watanabe, 1951, p. 429).

At the center of Tanabe Pharma's transformation was education. The company meticulously curated a rich spectrum of printed materials, ranging from introductory to advanced topics, to disseminate the nuances of QC. Tanabe Pharma's research institute assumed the mantle of guiding explorations into experimental design methods by holding seminars as a cornerstone of knowledge transfer. Collaborations with experts, including Prof. Sakamoto Heihachi of Kobe University, stimulated research on the infusion of advanced expertise into the educational landscape (Demingusho Iinkai, 1950, p. 11).

In 1949, another pivotal juncture took place during the production of the anti-TB drug NIPPAS. Confronted with the need for mass production because of the rise in daily consumption, Tanabe Pharma was guided by its dedication to QC. The Onoda factory at the time was a conducive setting for the transition, with dedicated efforts and collaboration supporting the successful realization of mass production (Demingusho Iinkai, 1950, p. 11).

Tanabe Pharma's organizational structure transformed its quest for optimal QC. Recognizing the need for dedicated focus, the company established its Quality Control Department in 1950, bolstered by a Quality Control Committee. The subsequent creation of its Market Research and Statistics Committee aligned with Deming's circle, which the company learned from Deming's eight-day lecture, and its holistic approach was supplemented by other related QC seminars (Demingusho Iinkai, 1950, p. 2).

The year 1951 marked a momentous achievement for Tanabe Pharma. Fueled by Deming's 1950 lectures, the company took a remarkable leap in terms of the quality of NIPPAS, which earned the distinction of becoming Japan's first Quality Control Product (QCP). These efforts culminated in Tanabe Pharma being conferred the inaugural Deming Prize (Demingusho Iinkai, 1950, pp. 7-8).

Tanabe Pharma's impact transcended industry as its developments led to a 50% reduction in Japan's TB mortality rate with other entities in the pharmaceutical industry in 1952. These accomplishments highlighted the company's unyielding dedication to QC and its profound influence on public health outcomes (Oda & Matsumoto, 2001, p. 164).

Tanabe Pharma's acceptance of QC and reception of the Deming Application Prize are testaments to its unwavering pursuit of excellence. From its historical roots to its pivotal role in shaping healthcare outcomes, Tanabe Pharma's legacy is etched in the history of industry and society.

4.7 Deming's Paradigm: Consumer Satisfaction and Cost Reduction through Statistical Quality Control

Deming's SQC sought to achieve both "consumer satisfaction" and cost reduction (Koyanagi, 1950b, p. 3). Contrary to the notion that cutting costs would diminish quality, Deming's SQC demonstrated that prioritizing higher-quality products could in fact reduce overall costs. This shift in perception from "cheap and nasty" to quality-driven items transformed Japan's business mindset and played a pivotal role in the nation's economic reconstruction and its eventual adoption in the United States (Asada, 1950, pp. 46-47).

Deming's SQC strategy, which featured the plan-do-check-act cycle, not only identified defects but also controlled quality during inspection. It embraced the statistical analysis of acceptable defective products and embraced variations within production processes while also advocating for continuous improvement and additional steps such as testing products in service (Koyanagi, 1950b, p. 10).

Deming's teachings highlighted that differences in quality were driven by systems rather than by individuals. His calculation of system-induced variation limits underscored management's role in improving systems to eliminate quality issues, forming a crucial aspect of his SQC strategy (Koyanagi, 1950b, pp. 13-18).

Tanabe Pharma's acceptance of SQC after Deming's seminar in 1950 coincided with Japan's postwar focus on producing profitable, high-quality goods at lower costs. Deming's promotion of consumer-oriented quality resonated with Tanabe Pharma, whose adoption of SQC led to significant productivity and quality improvements in products such as NIPPAS (Demingusho Iinkai, 1951, p. 1).

As Tanabe Pharma ventured into NIPPAS production, its use of Deming's SQC approach aligned with Japan's economic shift toward reliance on the private sector for medical services, marking a pivotal change in the company's strategy and outlook.

In 1952, the Deming Prize was awarded to Takeda Pharmaceutical Company Limited and Shionogi & Co., Ltd., which, along with other Japanese pharmaceutical companies, had obtained domestic manufacturing approval for SM from the MHW in July 1950. Takeda used control charts and sampling techniques in its penicillin production QC (Demingusho Iinkai, 1952, pp. 54-64). Shionogi also applied control charts and sampling methods in manufacturing vitamins tablets called "Paraesu-jo" to manage quality (Demingusho Iinkai, 1952, pp. 43-53).

About 400 participants expressed their intention to implement Deming's SQC after attending his lectures, including a session for 230 people in July 1950, a lecture for executives at Hakone Hotel and Tokyo's Nihon Industrial Club, and a session at Kyushu University in August (JUSE, 1997, pp. 29-33).

In 1954, another quality management expert, Joseph Moses Juran, visited Japan and introduced TQC as a comprehensive quality management approach, marking the inception of TQC (JUSE, 1997, pp. 40-42). Despite criticisms regarding issues such as excessive labor, these were not targeted at quality management itself (Nakayama, 1995b, pp. 273-274). The evolution of Japan's QC approach involved the incorporation of both Deming's and Juran's methodologies. Japan integrated and developed these quality management methods to shape its unique quality practices in collaboration with the four actors: governments, industries, universities, and civilians.

Chapter 5 The Pharmaceutical Industry in Occupied Japan

This chapter examines how the relation between the Japanese pharmaceutical industry and SQC, particularly the production of anti-TB drugs, has contributed to the reduction in TB mortality in Japan.

5.1 Evolution of Combination Therapy and Anti-TB Drug Manufacturing in Occupied Japan

Medical publications have described the effects of combination therapy with SM and PAS (Koseisho Imukyoku Kokuritsuryoyojokanai and Kokuritsuryoyojoshi Kenkyukai: MHW/Sanatoria, 1976, p. 162). PAS, however, was considered a secondary anti-TB drug by medical experts in occupied Japan that nevertheless helped lower the TB mortality rate after 1950 (Aldous & Suzuki, 2012, p. 151). In May 1950, Tanabe Pharma already obtained approval from the MHW to domestically manufacture and sell PAS as an anti-TB drug. This was two months earlier than five other Japanese companies, including Meiji Seika (Meiji Seika Pharma Co., Ltd. at present), were allowed to sell domestically produced SM in July 1950 (JSHP, 1995, pp. 248-251). Tanabe Pharma, which has imported pharmaceutical products worldwide since 1678, is the oldest private pharmaceutical company in Japan (Tanabe Seiyaku, 1983, p. 3).

Pharmaceutical companies in Japan initially declined to manufacture SM because they needed a large amount of facility investment and a high level of technology for fermentation equipment. In July 1950, Meiji Seika; Kyowa Hakko Kogyo Co., Ltd (Kyowa Hakko); Kaken Kagaku Co., Ltd. (Kaken Kagaku); Shimane Kagaku Co., Ltd. (Shimane Kagaku); and Nihon Seibutsu kenkyujo Co., Ltd. (Nihon Seibutsu Kenkyujo) were allowed to manufacture and sell SM in Japan (JSHP, 1995, p. 183).

The MHW purchased the first batch of domestic SM at the "First Domestic Streptomycin Purchase Ceremony" held on July 18, 1950. This included 1,160 one-gram (potency) bottles produced by 5 companies: Meiji Seika, Kagaku Kenkyujo (Kaken Kagaku), Nihon Bioscience Institute (Nikken Kagaku), Kyowa Hakko, and Shimane Kagaku. However, these five companies produced 116.6 kilograms of SM within 6 months in December 1950 (Yagisawa, Foster, & Kurokawa, 2015, pp. 131-142). The use of SM, however, was decreased since it caused hearing loss (Kitamoto & Fujita, 1953, pp. 49-50).

5.2 Regulatory Changes and Healthcare Expansion in Occupied Japan

The production volume of medicines increased by about 30% annually because of the special demand resulting from the Korean War, which broke out in 1950. There was a particular increase in the prices of target products (Tanabe Seiyaku, 1983, p. 191).

Regarding drug prices, the MHW abolished the "Rules for Production and Supply of Pharmaceutical Products and Sanitary Materials" in 1947 to control pharmaceutical products and sanitary materials. Instead, the

MHW established the "Rules for Supply of Pharmaceutical Products" (November 11, 1947) under the "Receipt Adjustment Act of Temporary Goods" (October 1, 1946). According to these rules, the MHW would control the distribution of 132 medical products, sanitary materials, and infant treatment medical items. The MHW released these controls sequentially and renewed the "Supply Regulation of Pharmaceutical Products" (July 3, 1950) in 1950 (Okurasho Insatsukyoku, 1950).

As stipulated in the above regulation, the MHW supplied controlled medical products through central distributors and local dealers in exchange for the purchase certificate of designated distribution goods issued by the MHW minister or prefectural governors. The MHW allocated supplies according to prefecture, and the prefectural governor issued purchase orders. In 1952, the MHW eased control, which meant end users could purchase products freely (MHW, 1976, p. 447).

On July 29, 1948, the government established the "Pharmaceutical Affairs Law," which provided detailed criteria for antimicrobial substance preparations, including penicillin, SM, and biological preparations (Okurasho Insatsukyoku, 1948). On March 1, 1951, the government promulgated the Sixth Revised Japanese Pharmacopoeia, which was based on the 13th edition of American Pharmacopoeia and an update from the Fifth Revised Japanese Pharmacopoeia called the "Wartime Pharmacopoeia" (Okurasho Insatsukyoku, 1951).

Patients have been able to use their social insurance for SM and PAS since 1950 (MHW, 1976, p. 474), which is essential because regular citizens under the "civilians" actor group who could not purchase the abovementioned drugs because of their high prices could now do so because of the "government" actor, which shouldered the drug costs via social insurance.

On March 31, 1951, the government enacted the Tuberculosis Prevention Act (Okurasho Insatsukyoku, 1951), which allowed TB patients to receive medical treatment at public expense starting October 1, 1951 (MHW, 1976, p. 474). However, the Pharmaceutical Society of Japan's amendment of the National Formulary, including the above anti-TB drugs, was delayed to March 1955 (MHW, 1976, pp. 447-450).

In April 1950, the House of Representatives and the House of Councilors passed resolutions to strengthen anti-TB measures. On November 16, 1950, the Shakaihosho Seido Shingikai (Council on Social Security System) issued recommendations regarding the social security system, which declared TB as a national disease and a major social problem. The council argued that the Japanese government and local government organizations should establish comprehensive and systematic countermeasures. The government responded to these recommendations by discussing measures against TB, but it was not until the following year, on April 1, 1956, that the new Tuberculosis Prevention Law went into effect (MHW, 1976, p. 474).

The private sector quickly addressed the above administrative delays. The following section outlines their activities.

5.3 Transformative Impact of Statistical Quality Control on Private Sector Pharmaceutical Supply: Quality, Quantity, and Financial Growth

In 1950, a stable and sustainable supply system for high-quality pharmaceutical products in the private sector was established as a result of the SQC approach (JSHP, 1995, p. 249). Following the enforcement of the Pharmaceutical Affairs Law in 1948, the pharmaceutical industry in

Japan adopted SQC in the production process of their primary medical products (JUSE, 1951, pp. 7-8). As a result, the pharmaceutical industry in Japan significantly improved product quality and volume and its production process while setting low prices. Tanabe Pharma won the first Deming Prize in 1951 and received a performance award from the MHW in 1952 for helping reduce the TB mortality rate in Japan by 50% (Tanabe Seiyaku, 2006).

In 1951, the TB mortality rate was 110.3 per 100,000, which was about half the rate in 1939 when Her Majesty the Empress conveyed her imperial message on the TB mortality rate. This improvement was caused by the dramatic decline in TB mortality among the youth and adult males (MHW, 1976, p. 475).

For the Japanese pharmaceutical industry and Tanabe Pharma, this case was significant because, at least in 1950, a supply system for larger volumes and higher-quality pharmaceutical products with lower prices was established in the private sector (JSHP, 1995, p. 249). In 1952, Takeda Pharmaceutical Co., Ltd. (Takeda Pharma) and Shionogi and Co., Ltd. (Shionogi Pharma) won the Deming Prize.

Next, Takeda Pharma adopted SQC in its production process and continued to improve the yield percentage of organic synthetic chemicals and penicillin and decreased substandard injection rates and products using their experimental design. Takeda's tangible improvements translated into a net annual turnover exceeding 100 million yen in 1951 (Demingusho Iinkai, 1952, pp.16-18).

Shionogi Pharma also improved its synthetic chemical yield rate and posted an annual turnover of 150 million yen. Turnover figures for its tablets division and injection division were 20 million yen and 80 million yen, respectively. In 1951, Shionogi's total annual turnover was 250 million yen (Demingusho Iinkai, 1952, pp. 15-16).

Data from the Ministry of International Trade and Industry showed that the pharmaceutical industry had 972 establishments in 1950 and 979 in 1951. The total amount of annual shipment, namely the annual turnover, of the pharmaceutical industry was around 32.3 billion yen in 1950 and 44.9 billion yen in 1951. Establishments averaged an annual turnover of 33.2 million yen in 1950 and 45.8 million yen in 1951 (MITI, 1961).

These figures show that the major pharmaceutical companies at that time, including Tanabe Pharma, Takeda Pharma, and Shionogi Pharma, posted much higher annual turnovers than smaller establishments in Japan. After 1950, these companies adopted the SQC method and achieved higher annual turnovers with the high-quality medical products that they specialized in with the enactment of the Tuberculosis Prevention Act (Act No. 96 of 1951) on March 31, 1951. Furthermore, in 1961, the Japanese Universal Health Insurance System, which sought to cover anti-TB drugs, including SM and PAS, was finally established (MHLW, 2011).

In July 1949, the American Pharmaceutical Association Mission came to Japan and recommended the separation of medical practice from pharmaceutical dispensing (Akiba et al., 2012, pp. 69-134), which was ineffective until April 1, 1956 (Akiba et al., 2012, pp. 69-134).

More than a decade passed before a stable supply of pharmaceutical products was realized through a general framework. In the private sector, Deming's SQC method contributed to the stability of the supply system for high-quality pharmaceutical products at least six years earlier than in the public sector.

5.4 Comparative Anti-TB Drug Strategies: Japan and the United States in the Mid-twentieth Century

This section examines different approaches against TB as Japan and the United States forged their anti-TB drug strategies.

5.4.1 Streptomycin Production

The *PHW Weekly Bulletin*, from October 14, 1945, to December 31, 1949, reported that a total of 200 and 400 kilograms of SM were distributed to pharmaceutical companies in Japan in July and October, respectively, not to hospitals. The distribution list for July was as follows: 53,197 grams to Takeda Yakuhin Kogyo KK (Takeda Pharma), 50,000 grams to Shionogi Seiyaku KK (Shionogi Pharma), 41,195 grams to Sanyo KK (Sanyo Pharma), 32,396 grams to Yamanouchi Seiyaku KK (Yamanouchi Pharma), and the remaining to Banyu Seiyaku KK (Banyu Pharma), albeit unconfirmed (Sugita & Suzuki, 2008). For October, the distribution list was as follows: 100,000 grams to Takeda Pharma; 50,000 grams to Shionogi Pharma; 30,000 grams to Tanabe Pharma; 30,000 grams to Fujisawa Yakuhin Kogyo Co., Ltd. (Fujisawa Pharma); 30,000 grams to Yamanouchi Pharma; 30,000 to Dainippon Seiyaku Co., Ltd. (Dainippon Pharma); 30,000 grams to Daiichi Seiyaku Co., Ltd. (Daiichi Pharma); 20,000 grams to Sankyo Pharma; 20,000 grams to Torii Seiyaku Co., Ltd. (Torii Pharma); 20,000 grams to Tokyo Tanabe Seiyaku Co., Ltd. (Tanabe Pharma, Tokyo); 20,000 grams to Banyu Pharma; and 20,000 grams to Nakamura Taki Shoten Co., Ltd. (Nakamura Taki Pharma) (Sugita & Suzuki, 2008).

In July 1950, Japanese private enterprises began domestically producing SM. In 1952, large factories in Japan succeeded in manufacturing the necessary quantities of SM. PAS was also produced as an anti-TB drug to assist the SM administered to TB patients. Although the TB mortality rate continuously declined from 1951 to 1953, the number of people infected with TB remained high.

In 1961, the TB infection rate was 445.9 per 100,000, which was still high after 10 years in Japan. Since venereal disease followed the same pattern as TB, this phenomenon was considered an "entrenched nature of the chronic infectious disease" (Aldous & Suzuki, 2012, p. 151).

In 1961, Japan had a total population of 94,285,000, of which more than 420,000 were infected with TB (MHW, 1976, p. 516). That year, a total of 27,916 people died of TB, with a mortality rate of 29.6 per 100,000 (MHW, 1976, p. 545). Overall, the number of people infected with TB was 10 times that of those who died of the disease.

5.4.2 Para-aminosalicylic Acid Production

On May 6, 1950, Japanese pharmaceutical companies, led by Tanabe Pharma, Takeda Pharmaceutical, and Shionogi Pharma, obtained government approval for the commercial production of PAS and began to manufacture the drug domestically. *In January 1950, before the commercial production approval*, these companies produced 565 kilograms of sodium *PAS, the most commonly produced and used form of PAS* (JSHP, 1995, p. 248).

The number of pharmaceutical companies increased to 15, and the PAS production volume reached 24,852 kilograms in December 1950, achieving a total of 141,232 kilograms for the year (GHQ/SCAP, 1952, pp. 211-212).

According to the 1950 National Health Insurance Drug Price Standard provided by the Minister of Health and Welfare, 100 grams of PAS cost 2,700 yen in 1950 (Nihon Seiyaku Dantai Rengokai: FPMAJ, 1950, p. 37).

In the same year, the market size of PAS rapidly grew to 3,813,264,000 yen. A patient required a daily dose of 10 grams of PAS. The 565-kilogram production volume in January 1950 corresponded to the volume required for 56,500 people per day. Production in Japan increased to a volume that can be administered to 14,123,300 people daily (GHQ/SCAP, 1952, p. 204).

The PHW employed penicillin experts. In 1946, the total production volume of penicillin was 100,000 Oxford units, equivalent to 23 vials. Three years later, the market size of penicillin reached 1,799,000,000 units, which cost 140 yen per 100,000 units for a total of 2,518,000,000 yen (Oxford University Press, 2017). In 1949, 38 licensed manufacturers produced penicillin in Japan (GHQ/SCAP, 1952, p. 204).

In 1949, the government excluded penicillin from distribution control products and, on October 1, cut all penicillin prices by about 50%. In 1950, when Deming introduced SQC in Japan and Takeda Pharmaceutical adopted SQC in its pharmaceutical manufacturing process, the annual production volume of penicillin reached 7,495,530,000 units, and its price dropped to 45 yen per 100,000 units, 32% from the previous fiscal year, although the market scale increased to 3,337,300,000 yen (GHQ/SCAP, 1952, p. 204).

5.4.3 Combination Therapy with Streptomycin and Para-aminosalicylic Acid

According to the National Sanatoria History Study Group, the first report of the Streptomycin Research Council in November 1949 described

SM administration as an intramuscular injection performed twice a day totaling 1 gram per day and discontinued the administration of up to 40 grams. This treatment was a short-term therapy.

Cases of mycobacterium TB dropped by about 50%. A survey found that 25% of patients died after finishing treatment (MHW/Sanatoria, 1976, p. 162). Tadao Shimao explained that the experts found that the combined treatment of SM and PAS could prevent the tolerance of SM. Physicians then started using SM and PAS to treat TB (Kekkakuyobokai, & Shimao, 2016, p. 98). According to the National Sanatoria History Study Group, in January 1951, the Streptomycin Research Council began a combination therapy of SM and PAS for the first time (MHW/Sanatoria, 1976, p. 162).

In the mid-twentieth century, the fight against TB was marked by evolving treatment paradigms and innovative drug combinations. Global efforts to combat this formidable disease can be explained through a comparison between the United States's 1951 approach and Japan's 1952 strategy (Kitamoto & Fujita, 1953, p. 1).

In 1951, the United States adopted a multifaceted anti-TB strategy. Understanding that chemotherapy alone was insufficient, its medical community emphasized the integration of medical and surgical treatments. One pivotal realization was the ability of combination therapy to delay the emergence of drug resistance. Here, the pairing of SM and PAS emerged as the gold standard because of their synergistic effect (Kitamoto & Fujita, 1953, pp. 7-8).

SM, which was considered the most potent anti-TB agent, proved most effective when combined with PAS. Intermittent administration every 2-3 days maintained efficacy while minimizing side effects. PAS functioned as a crucial companion to SM, especially in cases of SM resistance. The potential of SM was also explored alongside isonicotinic acid hydrazide to enhance efficacy (Kitamoto & Fujita, 1953, p. 8).

The prescription addressed a broad spectrum of TB manifestations, including pulmonary, genitourinary, and bone TB, with a tailored approach for each. Experts acknowledged the challenge of drug resistance and established resistance thresholds for effective treatment (Kitamoto & Fujita, 1953, pp. 8-9).

Meanwhile, Japan employed a precision treatment for early lesions. In 1952, the country's approach focused on early-stage lesions, which was a slightly different course from that of the United States. Japan strategically withheld chemotherapy when patients were expected to respond to systemic therapy or when collapse therapy was indicated. The preferred combination of SM and PAS balanced effectiveness, side effects, and tolerance (Kitamoto & Fujita, 1953, pp. 2-3).

SM and PAS emerged as the backbone of Japanese treatment, offering a versatile approach. SM could be used in isolation for limited resistance, while *sodium PAS* (NaPAS) monotherapy targeted specific scenarios. This nuanced approach extended to extrapulmonary TB complicated by late-stage pulmonary TB, for which tailored dosages were determined (Kitamoto & Fujita, 1953, pp. 3-4).

This approach was applied to a wide range of TB manifestations, from pulmonary and laryngeal to tracheobronchial and intestinal TB. The emphasis on combined surgery underscored the treatment's comprehensive nature (Kitamoto & Fujita, 1953, pp. 4-5).

As both countries grappled with drug resistance, they set resistance thresholds to gauge efficacy. Their anti-TB drug strategies reflected a dynamic period of medical exploration, and the collaborative use of various drugs and regimens to maximize efficacy while minimizing resistance highlights their nuanced understanding of TB treatment (Kitamoto & Fujita, 1953, pp. 13-15). These historical insights continue to inform modern anti-TB strategies, with emphasis on the importance of combination therapies, tailored dosages, and resistance monitoring in the ongoing battle against TB.

As discussed in the previous section, since 1950, each country has adopted almost the same chemotherapy as their TB treatment. This raises the question as to what other factors, besides chemotherapy, helped Japan reduce its TB mortality rate by 43.80% between 1950 and 1952.

5.5 Innovations and Challenges of the Pharmaceutical Industry in Occupied Japan

The "industry" of pharmaceuticals, which manufactured a mass volume of high-quality products at lower prices by applying the SQC method to the production process, led public health in occupied Japan, supported by the "government's" improvements in the legal system (Deming, 1987, pp. 489-492). Such developments in the "industry" through SQC had some challenging points. The government shouldered part of the people's medical expenses through universal healthcare. Consumers and the larger public, which belong to the "civilian" actor group, could frequently access high-quality medical care and pharmaceutical products.

However, the companies that adopted SQC encountered some problems because of their heavy dependence on its statistical methods. Their top management teams tended to lack a profound understanding of it (Nakayama, 1995b, p. 272).

Joseph M. Juran visited Japan in 1954 as a successor to Deming and presented a new perspective on the responsibility of management in quality and productivity improvement (Deming, 1985, Box #126). Juran, who held a QC course in Japan, advocated total companywide SQC while adhering to Deming's QC theory. This version of SQC was later criticized as a labor management issue that leads to death from overwork (Deming, 1985, Box #126).

SQC and the universal healthcare system significantly increased the number of people who could frequently access high-quality pharmaceutical products. This meant that people have experienced a society with both favorable and unfavorable elements in which they lived a long time with iatrogenic disease, drug-induced suffering, and intractable disease in an environment where all people have shared the paradox generated by advances in medical treatment (Sugiyama, 2010, p.292).

Chapter 6 Conclusion

This study has examined the transformative impact of the Japanese pharmaceutical industry's adoption of SQC on the reduction of the TB mortality rate in occupied Japan. Its comprehensive analysis of historical documents, governmental policies, industry practices, and medical advancements has clarified the crucial role played by collaborative partnerships among industries, universities, national and local governments, and civilians in enhancing public health in occupied Japan during a tumultuous period.

Deming's introduction of SQC was a turning point in Japan's postwar history. The collaboration among industries, universities, government agencies, and the civilian population led to the mass production of high-quality pharmaceutical products, specifically anti-TB drugs. Such collective effort was instrumental in curbing the high TB mortality rates that had plagued Japan for decades. By improving the quality, quantity, and affordability of anti-TB drugs, the pharmaceutical industry helped to substantially reduce TB-related deaths, which ultimately reshaped the public health trajectory in occupied Japan.

In addition, Tanabe Pharma's success is a noteworthy example of how SQC principles were incorporated into pharmaceutical manufacturing. By diligently implementing SQC methods, Tanabe Pharma achieved higher product quality, increased production capacity, and lowered costs.

By adopting SQC, Tanabe Pharma improved the availability of effective anti-TB drugs and set a standard that other pharmaceutical companies can follow. The recognition of Tanabe Pharma's efforts with the Deming Prize and Minister of Health and Welfare awards was demonstrative of the industry's commitment to excellence in product quality and public health.

Furthermore, this study has comparatively explored Japan's and the United States' anti-TB drug strategies in the mid-twentieth century. Although their goals are similar, their nuanced approaches clarify the multifaceted nature of TB treatment. Japan's emphasis on precision treatment for early lesions and the United States's multifaceted approach, including the adoption of combination therapies, highlighted the complexity of addressing TB in different contexts. Lessons learned from these strategies continue to inform modern efforts against TB, with emphasis on the significance of collaboration, tailored treatment, and resistance monitoring. Such efforts should be examined more as a future research challenge.

In conclusion, Deming's introduction of SQC to the pharmaceutical industry in occupied Japan transformed public health outcomes. The synergy between industry, academia, the government, and civilians fostered a dynamic environment in which a broader population could access high-quality medical products, which substantially lowered TB mortality rates. Such collaboration not only showcased the potential of SQC but also demonstrated the pivotal role of industry-academia-government partnerships in shaping a nation's health and well-being.

Reflecting on the history of Japan's pharmaceutical industry and its contributions to the decline in TB mortality, the author hopes that this dissertation serves as a reminder of the lasting impact of collaborative efforts on public health challenges, that is, the fight against infectious diseases both then and now.

Acknowledgments

I am grateful for the acknowledgement that this document was published with a publication grant from the Kyoto University of Foreign Studies. I sincerely thank the curators of the Library of Congress of the United States, the Archivist of the National Archives, the professors, primarily Professor Shuichi Shindo, who patiently provided thoughtful guidance, and the Daigaku Kyoiku Shuppan for their publication support.

References

Adachi, S. (2012a). *Beikoku ni okeru Byoin Genka Keisan no Hatten to Kachi Jushi no Byoin Keiei(Development of hospital cost accounting and value-oriented hospital management in the United States)* (dissertation). Fukuoka: Kyushu University.

Administrative Division, & Sams, C.F. Medical Care Aspects of Public Health and Welfare in Japan (Brig. Gen. Crawford F. Sams) (1949). *GHQ/SCAP Records.* Public Health and Welfare Section.

Adult Disease Department, Public Health Bureau, Ministry of Health and Welfare. (1979). *TB Annual Journal of Japan Antituberculosis Association*, Vol. 5. Tokyo: Ministry of Health and Welfare.

Akiba, Y., Nakamura, T., Nishikawa, A., & Watanabe, T. (2012). *Iyakubungyo no Rekishi: Shogen de Tsuzuru Nihon no Iyakubungyoshi (Separation History of Medical Practice from Pharmaceutical Dispensing)*. Tokyo: Yakujinipposha.

Aldous, C., & Suzuki, A. (2012). *Reforming Public Health in Occupied Japan, 1945-52: Alien Prescriptions?* Abingdon: Routledge.

Amakawa, A., & Sugiyama, A. (1996). *GHQ Nihon Senryoshi: Koshueisei (History of the Nonmilitary Activities of the Occupation of Japan, 1945-1951: Public Health)*, Vol. 22. Tokyo: Nihon Tosho Senta.

Amakawa, A., & Sugiyama, A. (1996). *Kaisetsu*. In Sugiyama, A. (Trans.). *GHQ Nihon Senryoshi: Koshueisei (History of the Nonmilitary Activities of the Occupation of Japan, 1945-1951: Public Health)*, (Vol. 22, 1-11). Tokyo: Nihon Tosho Senta.

Aoki, J. (2016). Nihon ni okeru Kekkakuryoyojo no Rekishi to Jiki Kubun ni Kansuru Kosatsu (A Study on period division of the history of the tuberculosis sanatorium in Japan). *Senshu Daigaku Shakaikagaku Nenpo Dai 50 (The 50th Social Science Annual Report of Senshu University)*, 50.

Aoki, M. (2003). *Kekkaku no Rekishi: Nihon Shakai tono Kakawari Sono Kako, Genzai, Mirai (History of Tuberculosis: Relation with Japanese Society, Its Past,*

Present and Future). Tokyo: Kodansha.

Aoki, M. (2008). Wagakuni no Kekkaku Taisaku no Genjo to Kadai-1: Wagakuni no Kekkaku Taisaku no Ayumi (Current TB Prevention Measures and Problems in Japan Part 1: History of TB Prevention Measures in Japan). *Nihon Koeishi*, 55(9).

Asada, G. (1950). Hinshitsu ga Kureimu no Genin to natta Yushutsuseihin. *Hinshitsukanri (Quality Control)*, 1(1).

Asao, M. (1950). Kagakukogyo deno Jikkenkeikakuho no Oyorei (Application Example of Experimental Planning in the Field of Chemical Industry). *Hinshitsukanri (Quality Control)*, 1(4).

Carr, E. Hallett (2014). In Shimizu, I. *(Translator), Rekishi towa nanika (In What is history?)*. Tokyo: Iwanami Shoten.

Cohen, T. (1983). *Nihon Senryo Kakumei: GHQ kara no Shogen = The Third Turn: MacArthur, the Americans and the Rebirth of Japan*. Tokyo: TBS Buritanika.

Dees, B. C. (1997). *The Allied Occupation and Japan's Economic Miracle Building the Foundations of Japanese Science and Technology* 1945-52 (1st ed.). Richmond: Japan Library. Retrieved from https://books.google.co.id/books/about/The_Allied_Occupation_and_Japan_s_Econom.html?id=Rci1AQAAQBAJ&redir_esc=y.

Deming, W.E. (1985). Out of Crisis. *Deming Papers*. Washington, DC: Library of Congress. Box.126.

Deming, W.E. (1950, August 4). Unpublished manuscript. *W.E. Deming Papers*. Washington: Library of Congress D.C. Box. 26.

Deming, W.E. (1950a). Keieisha ni Atau (for Company Managers). *Hinshitsukanri (Quality Control)*, 1(7).

Deming, W.E. (1950b). Tokeiteki Hinshitsukanri towa Nani ka (What Is Statistical Quality Control?). *Hinshitsukanri (Quality Control)* Miura, S. (Trans.), 1(6).

Deming, W.E. (1950c). Keieisha ni Atau (to Business Leaders). *Hinshitsukanri (Quality Control)*, 1(7).

Deming, W.E. (1952). *Demingu Hakushi Kogiroku Tokeiteki Hinshitsukanri no Kisoriron to Oyo (A Series of Lectures)*. Tokyo: JUSE. Retrieved from August 9,

2022. Retrieved from https://www.researchgate.net/publication/285255302.

Deming, W.E. (1987). *Letter from Deming to Mr. Noguchi, JUSE*. Unpublished manuscript. W.E. Deming Papers. Washington: Library of Congress D.C. Box.15.

Deming, W.E. (2000). *Out of the Crisis (Kindle)*. Cambridge, MA: MIT Press.

Demingusho Iinkai. (Deming Prize Committee) (1951). *1951nendo Demingusho narabini Demingusho Jisshisho Senko Riyusho (Deming Prize and Ground of Deming Prize Award in 1951)*. Tokyo: JUSE.

Demingusho Iinkai. (1952). Riyusho (Grounds of Deming Prize). In Demingusho Iinkai (Ed.), *1952nendo Demingusho Iinkai Hokoku narabini Demingusho Jisshisho Senko Riyusho (Grounds of Deming Prize and Deming Application Prize in 1952)*, 1-20. Tokyo: JUSE.

Dodge, J.M., & M.O.F. (1982). Memorandum:Summary of Meeting with Finance Minister Ikeda in 11-21 Japanese Government Budget. In *The Financial History of Japan: The Allied Occupation Period, 1945-1952. 20, English Documents (Showa Zaiseishi: Shusen kara Kowa made. 20, Eibun Shiryo)*, (Vol. 20, 757-760). Tokyo: Toyo Keizai Shimposha.

Dower, J.W. (1985). Yoshida Shigeru no Shiteki Ichizuke (Historical Assessment of Shigeru Yoshida). In R. Sodei (Ed.) *Hosei Daigaku Dai 8 kai Kokusai Shimpojiumu (the Eighth Hosei University International Symposium)* (1985th ed., 142-160). Tokyo: Nihon Hyoronsha.

Dower, J.W. (2000). *Embracing Defeat: Japan in the Wake of World War II*. New York: W.W. Norton & Company.

Economic Stabilization Board (ESB), Japan Government (1950, October). *Recent Trend of Japan's Economy, October 1950*. Retrieved from https://www.digital.archives.go.jp/DAS/meta/listPhoto?LANG=default&BID=F2007021516455907104&ID=&TYPE=dljpeg.

French, T. (2014). *National Police Reserve: The Origin of Japan's Self Defense Forces*. Danvers: Global Oriental

GHQ/SCAP (1948, December 18). Appendix 10:Memorandum for the Supreme Commander for Allied Powers from the Second US Scientific Mission to Japan.

In *GHQ/SCAP, History of the Nonmilitary Activities of the Occupation of Japan, 1945-1951: Reorganization of Science and Technology in Japan*. Tokyo: Nihon Tosho Senta.

GHQ/SCAP (1995). *GHQ Nihon Senryoshi:1945-1951(History of the Nonmilitary Activities of the Occupation of Japan, 1945-1951):Public Health* Takano, Y. (Ed.), Vol. VIII. Tokyo: Nihon Tosho Senta.

GHQ/SCAP Civil Historical Section (CHS). (1952). *History of the Nonmilitary Activities of the Occupation of Japan: Social Security*, Vol. 24. Tokyo: Nihon Tosho Senta.

GHQ/SCAP. (1952). Reorganization of Science and Technology in Japan. *History of the Nonmilitary Activities of the Occupation of Japan*, 1945-1951, Vol. 51. Tokyo: Nihon Tosho Senta.

GHQ/SCAP. (1990). *History of the Nonmilitary Activities of the Occupation of Japan 1945-1951: Public Health*, Vol. 22. Tokyo: Nihon Tosho Senta.

GHQ/SCAP. (1945). SCAPIN-1: General Order No. 1 (Directive No.1). Office of the Supreme Commander for the Allied Powers, 1945/09/02. Retrieved from https://dl.ndl.go.jp/info:ndljp/pid/9885063.

GHQ/SCAP. (1945). SCAPIN-2: General Order No. 2 (Directive No.2). Office of the Supreme Commander for the Allied Powers, 1945/09/03. Retrieved from https://dl.ndl.go.jp/info:ndljp/pid/9885064.

GHQ/SCAP. (1945). SCAPIN-47: Directive No.3. Office of the Supreme Commander for the Allied Powers, 1945/09/22. Retrieved from https://dl.ndl.go.jp/info:ndljp/pid/9885109.

Goto, M. (1950). Sekai no Hinshitsukanri 3 (Quality Control Works in World 3). *Hinshitsukanri (Quality Control)*, 1(5), 32-35.

Government of Japan (1947). Dai 25 Jo (Article 25). *Nihonkokukenpo (The Constitution of Japan)*. Retrieved from https://japan.kantei.go.jp/constitution_and_government_of_japan/constitution_e.html.

Hadley, E., & Sodei, R. (1985). *"1983nen kara Mita Senryoka no Keizai Kaikaku" Hosei Daigaku Dai 8 kai Kokusai Sympojiumu: Sekaishi no Naka no Nihon Senryo*. Tokyo: Nihon Hyoronsha.

Hein, L.E. (1993). Growth Verses Success: Japan's Economic Policy in Historical Perspective. In *Postwar Japan as History*. Berkeley: University of California Press. 109-110.

Ichikawa, H. (1987a). Chosen Senso Izen ni okeru Hinshitsukanri to Kanrigijiutsu no Donyu no Igi ni tsuite: GHQ no Tainichi Sangyo Seisaku no Shiten kara (Significance of Quality Control and Management Technology Before Korean War: GHQ's Industrial Policy in Occupied Japan). *Keieikenkyu (Business Studies)*, 38(5).

Ichikawa, H. (1987b). GHQ Kagakugijutsuka no Seisaku to Katsudo ni tsuite (Policy and Activities of ESS/GHQ in Occupied Japan). *Osakashidai Ronshu*. Osaka City University papers.

Igarashi, T. (2005). Senryoka Nihon no Kokusaiteki Chii (International Position of Occupied Japan). In M. Nakamura, A. Amakawa, K. Yun, & T. Igarashi (Eds.) *Sengo Nihon: Senryo to Sengo Kaikaku* (Post-war Japan: Occupation and Post-war Reformation) , 125-159. Tokyo: Iwanami Shoten.

Inao, M. (1950). Sokan ni Yosete: Sumiyakani Jisshi o (Address: I Recommend the Prompt QC Implementation). *Hinshitsukanri (Quality Control)*, 1(1), 4.

Iokibe, M. (1985a). *Beikoku no Nihon Senryo Seisaku: Sengo Nihon no Sekkeizu-Jokan (the U.S. Occupation Policy in Japan: A Blueprint for Postwar Japan-Vol.1)*. Tokyo: Chuo Koronsha.

Iokibe, M. (1985b). *Beikoku no Nihon Senryo Seisaku: Sengo Nihon no Sekkeizu-Gekan (the U.S. Occupation Policy in Japan: A Blueprint for Postwar Japan-Vol.2)*. Tokyo: Chuo Koronsha.

Irie, A. (1978). *Nichibei Senso (Japan-US War)*. Tokyo: Chuo Koronsha.

Ishikawa, I. (1950a). Preface. *Hinshitsukanri (Quality Control)*, 1(1).

Ishikawa, I. (1950b). Shinjidai no Keieisha eno Kitai: Hinshitsukanri Hoshiki Hatten no Dai 2 dankai ni tsuite (Expectation for New Age Owner: About the Second Stage of Quality Control Development). (JUSE, Ed.). *Hinshitsukanri (Quality Control)*, 1(4).

J.S.S.P. (Nihon Yakushi Gakkai [The Japanese Society for History of Pharmacy:JSHP]) (1995). Dai 4 bu Iyakuhin Kaihatsu no Kiroku (Chapter 4

Development History of Healthcare Products). *Nihon Iyakuhin Sangyoshi (Industry History of Healthcare Products in Japan)*. Tokyo: Yakuji Nipposha.

JUSE. (1950a). General Principles. *Hinshitsukanri (Quality Control)*, 1(1).

JUSE. (1950b). Editorial Direction. *Hinshitsukanri (Quality Control)*, 1(1).

JUSE. (1950c). Welcome Dr. Deming: 7gatsu 10,11, 12, 13, 14, 15, 17 and 18 nichi renzoku 8kkan. *Demingu Hakushi ni yoru Hinshitsukanri Koshukai* (Welcome Dr. Deming: Quality Control Seminar for serial eight days from July 10 to 18. Enjiniakurabu (Engineer Club), No27.

JUSE. (1950d). Demingu Hakushi ga Ataerareta Mono (What Did Dr. Deming Give Us?). *Hinshitsukanri (Quality Control)*, 1(6), 1.

JUSE. (1950e). Demingu Hakushi ni yoru Hinshitsukanri Koshukai (Lectures on Quality Control by Dr. Deming). *Hinshitsukanri (Quality Control)*, 1(4)d.

JUSE. (1951). Demingu Hakushi to Tomoni (Together with Dr. Deming). *Hinshitsukanri (Quality Control)*.

JUSE. (1997). Soritsu Gojunenshi (50 -Year Chronicle). Tokyo: JUSE.

JUSE. (2015). Tokeiteki Hinshitsukanri no Rekishi (History of Statistical Quality Control). *Nihon Kagakugijutsu Renmei (Union of Japanese Scientists and Engineers)*. Retrieved from https://www.juse.or.jp/statistical/history/.

JUSE. (2023). Winners List. *Nihon Kagakugijutsu Renmei (Union of Japanese Scientists and Engineers)*. Tokyo: JUSE. Retrieved from https://www.juse.or.jp/deming_en/winner/.

Kawada, T., Nishibori, E., Sakamoto, H., & Goto, M. (1950). Demingu Hakushi o Mukaeru ni Atatte (to Welcome Dr. Deming). *Hinshitsukanri (Quality Control)*, 1(4).

Keizai Antei Honbu (Economic Stabilization Board). (1952a). *Showa 25 rekinen Kokuminshotoku Chosa Hokoku (Survey Report of National Income in 1950)*. Retrieved from http://www.esri.cao.go.jp/jp/sna/data/data_list/kakuhou/files/rekishi/pdf/2701_1.pdf.

Keizai Antei Honbu (Economic Stabilization Board). (1952b). *Showa 26 rekinen Kokuminshotoku Chosa Hokoku (Survey Report of National Income in 1951)*. Retrieved from http://www.esri.cao.go.jp/jp/sna/data/data_list/kakuhou/files/

rekishi/pdf/2706_1.pdf.

Keizai Antei Honbu (Ed.). (1998). *Rinjibusshijukyuchoseiho:showa 21nen Horitsu Dai 32 go (Act of Temporary Goods Supply and Demand Adjustment: Act No. 32 of 1949)*. Retrieved from http://www.geocities.jp/nakanolib/hou/hs21-32.htm.

Keizaishingicho. (1953). *Showa27nendo Kokuminshotoku Hokoku (Survey Report of National Income in 1952)*. Retrieved from http://www.esri.cao.go.jp/jp/sna/data/data_list/kakuhou/files/rekishi/pdf/2810_1.pdf.

Kekkakuyobokai, & Shimao, T. (2016). Dai 3 sho Kekkaku Taisaku:*Koshueisei no Rekishi*, 4 Sutoreputomaishin nado Kagakuryohozai no Shutsugen (4.Introduction of Chemotherapeutic Agent Including Streptomycin of Chapter 3 Measures Against Tuberculosis: History of Public Health). *Shogen de Tsuzuru Kekkaku Taisaku: Koshueisei no Rekishi (Testimony on Tuberculosis Control: History of Public Health in Japan)*. Tokyo: Kekkakuyobokai.

Kekkakuyobokai. (1993). *Kekkaku Tokei Soran 1900-1992 nen (Tuberculosis Statistics from 1900 to 1992)*. Tokyo: Kekkakuyobokai.

Kennan, G. F. (2000). Amerika Gaiko 50 nen (American Diplomacy: 1900-1950). Trans. Kondo, S., Iida, T., and Aruga, T. Tokyo: Iwanami Shoten.

Kim, N. (2002). The Foundation of GHQ/SCAP, PHW and the Occupation Policy (Part 2). *The Journal of Kyushu University of Nursing and Social Welfare*, 4(1).

Kitamoto, O, & Fujita, S. (1953). *Kekkaku no Kagakuryoho (Chemotherapy for Tuberculosis)*. Tokyo: Igaku Shoin. [National Diet Library Digital Collection version] doi: 10.11501/1377511.

Koseisho I. (Medical Affairs Bureau, Ministry of Health and Welfare). (1955a). Eisei Tokei (Healthcare Statistics). *Isei Hachijunenshi (Eighty-year History of Healthcare System in Japan)*. Tokyo: Insatsukyoku Choyokai.

Koseisho I. (Medical Affairs Bureau, Ministry of Health and Welfare). (1958). *Eisei Gyosei Taiyo (Public Health Administration Summary)*. Tokyo: Nihon Koshu Eisei Kyokai.

Koseisho Imukyoku Kokuritsuryoyojokanai and Kokuritsuryoyojoshi Kenkyukai: MHW/Sanatoria. (1976). *Kokuritsuryoyojoshi (History of National Sanatorium)*. Tokyo: Zaidanhojin Koseimondai Kenkyukai.

Koyanagi, K. (1950a). Kojokeiei to Tokeiteki Hinshitsukanri (Factory Management and Statistical Quality Control). *Hinshitsukanri (Quality Control)*1(1).

Koyanagi, K. (1950b). *Dr. W. E. Deming's Lectures on Statistical Control of Quality*. Tokyo: Nihon Kagakugijutsu Renmei (Union of Japanese Scientists and Engineers: JUSE).

Koyanagi, K. (1950c). Participants List in the Deming SQC Seminar in 1950. *Deming Papers*. Washington DC: Library of Congress, the United States. Box 26.

Koyanagi, K. (1950d). Preface. *Dr. W. E. Deming's Lectures on Statistical Control of Quality*. Tokyo: JUSE.

Koyanagi, K. (1951a). Participants List in the Deming SQC Seminar in 1951. *Deming Papers*. Washington DC: Library of Congress, the United States, Box. 26.

Koyanagi, K. (1952). Participants List in the Deming SQC Seminar in 1952. *Deming Papers*. Washington DC: Library of Congress, the United States, Box. 26.

Koyanagi, K. (1997). Demingu Hakushi no Rainichi Yosei (Invitation for Dr. Deming to Japan). *Soritsu 50 Shunenshi (50 Anniversary of JUSE)*. Tokyo: JUSE.

Koyanagi, K. (Ed.). (1951c, August 3). *Enjinia Kurabu (Engineer Club)*. Tokyo: JUSE.

Matsuda, T. (2008). *Sengo Nihon ni okeru Amerika no Sofuto Pawa: Haneikyuteki Izon no Kigen (American Soft Power after World War II: Origin of Long-Term Dependence)*. Tokyo: Iwanami Shoten.

McCormick, T. J. (1992). *Pakusu Amerikana no Gojunen: Sekai Shisutemu no Naka no Gendai Amerika Gaiko (America's Half-Century:United States Foreign Policy in the Cold War)*. (T. Matsuda, A. Takahashi, & Y. Sugita, Trans.). Tokyo: Tokyo Sogensha.

Meiji Seika. Kabushikigaisha. (1987). *Meiji Seika no Ayumi: Sogyo kara 70 nen, 1916-1986 (History of Meiji Seika: 70 Years since Its Foundation. 1916-1986)*. Tokyo: Meiji Seika.

Ministry of Economy, Trade and Industry. METI. (2014). Kogyo Tokei 1950 (Industrial Statistics in 1950). *METI*. Retrieved from http://www.meti.go.jp/

statistics/tyo/kougyo/archives/index.html.
MHLW. (1948). Yobosesshuho (Immunization Act). *MHLW*. Retrieved from https://www.mhlw.go.jp/web/t_doc?dataId=79015000&dataType=0&pageNo=1.
MHW. (1950). *Kosei Daijin no Sadameru Yakka Kijun (Drug Price Standard. Established by Minister of Health and Welfare)*. Tokyo: Yakuji Nipposha.
MHW. (1953). *Nihon Yakkyokuho (Pharmacopoeia Japonica)* 6th ed. Tokyo: Koseisho (MHW).
MHW. (1955). *Isei Hachijunenshi (Eighty Years' History of the Medical System)*. Tokyo: Insatsukyoku Choyokai.
MHW. (1976a). *Isei Hyakunenshi (One Hundred Years' History of the Medical System)*. Tokyo: Gyosei.
MHW. (1976b). *Isei Hyakunenshi Shiryohen (One Hundred Yeares' History of the Medical System-Materials)*. Tokyo: Gyosei.
MHW. (2004a). Kekkakuyoboho : Showa 26 nen Horitsu Dai 96 go (TB Control Act:No. 96 Act in 1951). *Shugiin*. Retrieved from https://www.shugiin.go.jp/internet/itdb_housei.nsf/html/housei/15920040623133.htm.
MHW. (2005). Kanpo (July 3, 1950): Koseishorei dai36go (Official Gazette:MHW; Ordinance No. 36, July 3, 1950). Shugiin. Retrieved from http://dl.ndl.go.jp/info:ndljp/pid/2963587.
MHW. (1958). *Eisei Gyosei Taiyo (Summary of Public Health)*. Tokyo: Nihon Koshueisei Kyokai.
Ministry of Health and Welfare: MHW. (1949). Kekkakusho no Sutoreputomaishin Ryoho (TB Treatment; Streptomycin). (PHW, Ed.). *Nihon Iji Shimpo (Japanese Medical Journal)*. (1305).
Ministry of Health, Labour and Welfare: MHLW. (2011). Shakaihosho no Kensho to Tenbo. *MHLW*. Retrieved from http://www.mhlw.go.jp/wp/hakusyo/kousei/11/.
Ministry of International Trade and Industry. MITI. (1961). *Kogyo Tokei 50 nenshi 1909-1968 (History of the census of manufactures for 1909-1958)*. Tokyo: Okurasho Insatsukyoku.
MITI. (1991). *Tsusho Sangyo Seisakushi: Dai I Ki Sengo Fukkoki (1) (Policy History of International Trade and Industry: The first stage of Postwar Reconstruction*

(1)) (Vol. 2). Tokyo: Tsusho Sangyo Chosakai.
Ministry of Justice. Japan. (2009). Nihonkokukenpo (the Constitution of Japan). *Ministry of Justice* Retrieved from http://www.japaneselawtranslation.go.jp/law/detail_main?id=174.
Naikaku. (2019). *Chiikihokenho (Public Health Law)*. Retrieved from https://elaws.e-gov.go.jp/document?lawid=323CO0000000077.
Nakamura, M., & Takemae, E. (2005). GHQ-ron:Sono Soshiki to Kaikakushatachi (GHQ Study: Organization and Reformers). *Senryo to Kaikaku (Occupation and Reforms)*. Tokyo: Iwanami Shoten.
Nakamura, M., Amakawa, A., Yun, K., & Nakayama, S. (2005). Kagakugijutsu Rikkoku (Scientific and Technological Nation). *Sengo Kaikaku to Sono Isan (Post-war Reforms and Their Heritage)*. Iwanami Shoten.
Nakayama, S., Goto, K., Yoshioka, H., & Nakayama, S. (1995a). Gakujutsutaisei no Saihen (The Reorganization of Research Structure). *Tsushi Nihon no Kagakugijutsu (The Social History of Science and Technology in Contemporary Japan)*. (Vol. 1). Tokyo: Gakuyo Shobo.
Nakayama, S. (1995b). Hinshitsukanri no Nihonteki Tenkai (the Development of Japanese Style Quality Control). In S. Nakayama, K. Goto & H. Yoshioka (Eds.) *Tsushi Nihon no Kagakugijutsu 1945-1952 (The Social History of Science and Technology in Contemporary Japan: 1945-1952)*. (Vol. 1). Tokyo: Gakuyo Shobo.
Nakayama, S. (1995c). Saiensu Misshonzu no Rainichi (the Role of Advisory Missions). In S. Nakayama, K. Goto & H. Yoshioka (Eds.). *Tsushi Nihon no Kagakugijutsu Senryoki 1945-1952 (History of Japanese Science and Technology in Occupied Japan 1945-1952)*. (Vol. 1). Tokyo: Gakuyo Shobo.
National Institute of Infectious Diseases, Japan: NIID. (1998). *Kekkaku no Hoteki Toriatsukai no Hensen (Transition of TB Control Act)*. N.I.I.D. Retrieved from https://www.niid.go.jp/niid/ja/iasr-sp/2414-related-articles/related-articles-454/7726-454r01.html.
Nishibori, E. (1950). Korekara no Gijutsusha no Arikata (What Engineers Should Do?). *Hinshitsukanri (Quality Control)*, 1(1).

Nishimura, S. (2009). Promoting Health in American-Occupied Japan Resistance to Allied Public Health Measures, 1945-1952. *American Journal of Public Health*, 99(8), 1364-1375. doi: 10.2105/AJPH.2008.150532.

Nishizaki, F. (2022). *Amerika Gaikoshi (A History of American Foreign Relations)*. Tokyo Daigaku Shuppankai.

O'Brien, W. (1946, December 29). As Cited in Nakayama, 1995b, 270. *Japanese Standards Agency Holds Vital Industrial Role. Nippon Times*.

Oda, N., & Matsumoto, K. (2001a). NIPPAS 50 nen no Rekishi (Fifty-Year History of NIPPAS). *Yakushigaku Zasshi*, 36.

Okurasho Insatsukyoku. (Ed.) (1948, July 29). *Kampo (Official Gazette) [National Diet Library Digital Collection]*. Retrieved from https://dl.ndl.go.jp/pid/2962994/1/1. doi: 10.11501/2962994.

Okurasho Insatsukyoku. (Ed.) (1950, July 3). *Kampo (Official Gazette) [National Diet Library Digital Collection]*. Retrieved from http://dl.ndl.go.jp/info:ndljp/pid/2963587. doi: 10.11501/2963587

Okurasho Insatsukyoku. (Ed.) (1951, March 1). *Kampo (Official Gazette) [National Diet Library Digital Collection]*. Retrieved from http://dl.ndl.go.jp/info:ndljp/pid/2963788. doi: 10.11501/2963788

Okurasho Insatsukyoku. (Ed.) (1951, March 31). *Kampo (Official Gazette) [National Diet Library Digital Collection]*. Retrieved from http://dl.ndl.go.jp/info:ndljp/pid/2963813. doi:10.11501/2963813

Ouchi, H. (1950). Sokan ni Yosete:Tokei to Kogyo no Ketsugo o Yorokobu (Address: I am pleased to see collaboration between statistics and factory industry). *Hinshitsukanri (Quality Control)*, 1(1).

Oxford University Press (2017). Oxford Unit | Definition of Oxford Unit in English by Oxford Dictionaries. *Oxford Dictionaries | English*. accessed June 8, 2017. Retrieved from https://en.oxforddictionaries.com/definition/oxford_unit.;"Oxford unit" is "A unit of penicillin dosage originally adopted at the Sir William Dunn School of Pathology in the University of Oxford."

Patterson, R. P., the First Scientific Advisory Group, & the United States National Academy of Sciences (1947). Letter from Robert P. Patterson, Secretary of War to Dr. Frank B. Jewett, President National Academy of Sciences, The United States. *Reorganization of Science and Technology in Japan* (pp. i-viii). foreword. Tokyo: National Academy of Sciences of the United States of America.

Pharmaceuticals and Medical Devices Agency (2014, February 21). Yakuji Shokuhin Eisei Shingikai ni oite Kochi Shinsei ni Kakaru Jizen Hyoka ga Shuryoshi, Sonogo Yakuji Shonin Sareta Iyakuhin (Pharmaceutical Approved Medicines after the Pre-evaluation for Public Application by the Pharmaceutical Affairs / Food Sanitation Council). *Pharmaceutical and Medical Devices Agency.* Retrieved from http://www.pmda.go.jp/review-services/drug-reviews/review-information/p-drugs/0015.html

Rengokai, N. (1950). *Kosei Daijin no Sadameru Yakka Kijun (National Health Insurance (NHI) Drug Price Standard in 1950 Provided by the Minister of Health and Welfare).* Tokyo: Nihon Seiyaku Dantai Rengokai (FPMAJ).

Research Institute of Tuberculosis, & Japan Anti-Tuberculosis Association. JATA (2008). Kekkaku Taisaku no Genjo to Kadai (Current status and challenge). *Wagakuni no Kekkaku Taisaku no Genjo to Kadai(1) Wagakuni no, Kekkaku Taisaku no Ayumi (Current Status and Challenge of TB Policy in Japan (1): History of TB Policy in Japan)*, 55(9), 667-670. Retrieved from http://www.jata.or.jp/

Sakamoto, H. (1950). Demingu Hakushi o Mukaeru ni Atatte (Welcome Dr. Deming). *Hinshitsukanri (Quality Control)*, 1(4).

Sams, C. F. (1998). *DDT Kakumei: Senryoki no Iryofukushi Seisaku o Kaisosuru (Medic: The Mission of an American Military Doctor in Occupied Japan and War-torn Korea).* Trans. E. Takemae. Iwanami Shoten.

Sams, C. F. (2007). *GHQ Samusujunsho no Kaikaku: Sengonihon no Iryofukushiseisaku no Genten (Medic: The Mission of an American Military Doctor in Occupied Japan and War-torn Korea).* Trans. E. Takemae. Tokyo: Kiri Shobo.

Sams, C. F., & Zakarian, Z. (1998a). *Medic: The Mission of an American Military Doctor in Occupied Japan and War-torn Korea.* Armonk, NY: M.E. Sharpe.

Sams, C. F. (1949). Medical Care Aspects of Public Health and Welfare in Japan.

Journal of the American Medical Association. Reprinted by National Diet Library, Japan, 141(8), 527-531.

Sanger, D. E. (1990, March 3). Tokyo Tries to Find Out If "Salarymen" Are Working Themselves to Death. *New York Times*. New York. In *Deming Papers*. Washington, DC: Library of Congress. Box.126.

Sato, A. (2014). Public health improvement in Occupied Japan by W. Edward Deming: Statistical quality control (SQC) and anti-TB drug. *Doshisha Amerika Kenkyu (Doshisha American Studies), Special Issue*, 129-149.

Sato, A. (2016). Public Health in Occupied Japan Transformed by Statistical Quality Control. In Y. Sugita (Ed.), *Social Commentary on State and Society in Modern Japan*. Singapore: Springer, 67-82.

Sato, A. (2020). Reorganization of Science and Technology in Occupied Japan: Conformity to the Global Standard. *Journal of Osaka University of Tourism*, 20, 41-55. doi:10.20670/00000260.

Sato, A. (2021). Domestic production of anti-TB drugs in Occupied Japan. *Journal of Osaka University of Tourism, 23*, 53-62.

Schaller, M. (2004). *Nichibei Kankei towa Nan datta noka: Senryoki kara Reisen Shuketsugo made (Altered States: The United States and Japan Since the Occupation)*. Tokyo: Soshisha 99.

Shewhart, W. A., & Shirosaki, F. (1951). *Kogyoseihin no Keizaiteki Hinshitsukanri (Statistical Method: From the Viewpoint of Quality Control)*. Tokyo: Nihon Kikaku Kyokai.

Souers, S. W. (1948). Recommendations with Respect to U.S. Policy toward Japan (NSC13/2) Issued on October 7, 1948. *National Diet Library. Japan*. Retrieved from http://www.ndl.go.jp/modern/e/img_r/M008/M008-001r.html

Sugita, S., & Suzuki, A. (2008). Weekly Bulletin Public Health and Welfare Section. *GHQ, SCAP*: October 14, 1945 to December 31, 1949. Retrieved from http://www.rekishow.org/GHQ-PHW/material.html.

Sugita, Y. (1999). *Hegemoni no Gyakusetsu:Ajia Taiheiyo Senso to Beikoku no Higashiajia Seisaku 1945nen-1952nen (Paradoxes of Hegemony: The Asia-Pacific War and U.S. East Asian Policy, 1945-1852)*. Kyoto: Sekaishisosha.

Sugita, Y. (2008). 1950 nen "Shakaihosho Seido ni Kansuru Kankoku" no Saikento (Reviewing the "Recommendation for a Social Security System" in 1950). In *Nichibei no Iryo: Seido to Rinri (Medical in the United States and Japan: Systems and Ethics)*. Suita: Osaka Daigaku Shuppankai.

Sugita, Y., & Sugiyama, A. (2010). Chiiki ni okeru Shakaihosho Sisutemu (Local Social Security System). *Nichibei no Shakaihosho to Sono Haikei (Social Security in Japan and the U.S. and Its Background)*. Okayama: Daigaku Kyoiku Shuppan.

Sugiyama, A. (1995). *Senryoki no Iryo Kaikaku (Healthcare Reforms in Occupied Japan)* (dissertation). Tokyo: Tokyo Toritsu Daigaku.

Sugiyama, H. (1978). Hinsitsukanri to Onkochishin: Watashi to Demingu Hakushi tono 30 nen (Quality Control and the New Learning from the Past: My 30 Years with Dr. Deming). *Seisan to Gijutsu (Manufacturing and Technology)*.

Takeda, S. (2002). *Demingu no Soshikiron: Kankeichi Jidai no Makuake (Organization Theory of Deming: Commencement of Relationship on Knowledge)*. Tokyo: Toyo Keizai Shimposha.

Takemae, E. (1986). Kaisetsu (Explanation). *DDT kakumei: Senryoki no Iryofukushi Seisaku o Kaisosuru (Medic: The Mission of an American Military Doctor in Occupied Japan and War-torn Korea)*. Tokyo:Iwanami Shoten.

Takemae, E., & Imaizumi, M. (1996). *GHQ Nihon Senryoshi Josetsu (Preface of History of the Nonmilitary Activities of the Occupation of Japan 1945-1951)* (Vol. 1). Tokyo: Nihon Tosho Senta.

Takemae, E., Nakamura, T., & Amakawa, A. (1996). History of the *Nonmilitary* Activities of the Occupation of Japan, 1945-1951: Reorganization of Science and Technology in Japan. (Vol. 51). Tokyo: Nihon Tosho Senta.

Takemae, E., Nakamura, T., & Sugiyama, A. (1992). Kaisetsu. In Sugiyama, A. (Trans.). *GHQ Nihon Senryoshi, Koshueisei (GHQ Tokyo: the Occupation Headquarters and Its Influence on Postwar Japan, Public Health)* (Vol. 22). Tokyo: Nihon Tosho Senta.

Takemae, E., Nakamura, T., Amakawa, A., Ara, T., & Sanwa, R. (2000). *GHQ Nihon Senryoshi. Nihon no Kagakugijutsu no Saihen (History of the Nonmilitary*

Activities of the Occupation of Japan, 1945-1951: Reorganization of Science and Technology in Japan) (Vol. 51). Tokyo: Nihon Tosho Senta.

Takeuchi, T. (2011). Chugoku no Taito to Nichibei Domei no Taio (The Rise of China and the Correspondence of the Japan-US Alliance). In T. Takeuchi (Ed.), *Nichibei Domei-ron: Rekishi, Kino, Shuhen Shokoku no Shiten (US-Japan Alliance Theory: History, Functions, Perspectives of Neighboring Countries)*. Kyoto: Minerva Shobo.

Takeuchi, T., & Nakajima, H. (2011). Chiteki Koryu ni Miru Senzen Sengo-Shoki Nichibei Kankei no Danzetsu to Keizoku (Interruption and Continuation of the Early US-Japan Relations of Pre/Post World War II Observed in the Intellectual Exchange by Both Countries). In *Nichibei Domei-ron: Rekishi, Kino, Shuhen Shokoku no Shiten (US-Japan Alliance Theory: History, Functions, Perspectives of Neighboring Countries)*. Kyoto: Minerva Shobo.

Tanabe Seiyaku (1983). *Tanabe Seiyaku Sanbyakugonenshi (Three-Hundred-and-Five Year History of Tanabe Pharma)*. Osaka: Tanabe Seiyaku Kabushikigaisha.

Tanabe Seiyaku (2006). Tanabe Seiyaku Kabushikigaisha CSR Repoto 2006 (CSR Report 2006 by Tanabe Pharmaceutical Co., Ltd.). *Tanabe Seiyaku* Retrieved from http://www.mt-pharma.co.jp/csr/report/tanabe/pdf/2006_all.pdf.

The State-War-Navy Coordinating Committee: SWNCC (2003). United States Initial Post-surrender Policy for Japan (SWNCC150/4) of 6 September 1945. *National Diet Library. Japan*. Retrieved from http://www.ndl.go.jp/constitution/shiryo/01/022/022tx.html.

The United States, Army Service Forces (1943). *Civil Affairs Handbook: Japan*. vol. 13. Washington: United States Army Service Force.

The United States, Army Service Forces (1945). *Civil Affairs Handbook, Japan*. Washington, DC: Headquarters, Army Service Forces.

The United States National Academy of Sciences, T. F. S. A. G. (1947). *Reorganization of Science and Technology in Japan*. Tokyo: National Academy of Sciences of the United States of America.

The United States National Academy of Sciences, T. S. S. A. G. (1952). Memorandum for the Supreme Commander for the Allied Powers from the

Second Scientific Mission to Japan. *History of the Non-military Activities of the Occupation of Japan, 1945-1951: Reorganization of Science and Technology in Japan* (Vol. 51). GHQ/SCAP.

Truman, H. S. (1949). *Joseph M. Dodge Papers*. Washington: White House. Detroit: Detroit Public Library.

United Nations (1948). Article 25. Ministry of Foreign Affairs of Japan. Retrieved from https://www.mofa.go.jp/policy/human/univers_dec.html.

Walton, M. (1987). *Demingushiki Keiei (The Deming Management Method)*. Ishikawa, K. (Ed.) (Trans.) Kumagai, K. Tokyo: Purejidentosha. 20-25.

Watanabe, E. (1951). Amerika Senji Kikaku Z1: Hinshitsukanri Hoshiki no Kaisetsu (American Wartime Standard Z1: Explanation of Quality Control Methods. *Hinshitsukanri (Quality Control.)*, 2(9). Tokyo: JUSE.

Watanabe, M. (2009). Iryoshi kara Mita Sengoki no Yobosesshuho to Kekkakuyoboho no Kenkyu: Heisei 17 nendo—Heisei 20 nendo Kagaku Kenkyuhi Hojokin (Kiban Kenkyu (C)) *Kenkyu Seika Hokokusho (Study on Immunization Law and Tuberculosis Prevention Law in Occupied Japan from the View of Medical History*. Juntendo Daigaku Iryo Kango Gakubu.

Watanabe, M., Suzuki, A., Sakamoto, N., & Nagashima, T. (2008). *Kindainihon ni okeru Iryo no Yukosei to Risuku no Kenkyu:Iryo Seisaku no Tenkan to Nihonshakai no Taio ni tsuite (Kyodokenkyu Dai3kai Iryokango Kenkyukai)[A Study on the Effectiveness and Risk of Healthcare in Modern Japan: Transformation of Healthcare Policy and Response of Japanese Society, (Collaborative Research, The 3rd Healthcare Nursing Study Group)]*. Retrieved from https://ci.nii.ac.jp/naid/110006966317.

Yagisawa, M., Foster, P. J., & Kurokawa, T. (2015). Wagakuni ni oite Koseibusshitu Iyakuhin no Hinshitsu Kijun no Hatashita Yakuwari ni Kansuru Yakushigakuteki, Koshueiseigakuteki Kosatsu: Dainihon Penishirin oyobi Sutoreputomaishin no Kokusanka no Tassei (Historical and Hygienic Aspects on Roles of Quality Requirements for Antibiotic Products in Japan: Part 2 - Achievements of Domestic Production of Penicillin and Streptomycin). *The Japanese Journal for History of Pharmacy*. 50(2).

Yamagishi, T. (2010). Amerika Ishikai to Iryohoken (American Medical Association and Healthcare insurance Program" In *Nichibei no Shakaihosho to Sono Haikei (Social Security Program in Japan and the United States and Its Back Ground)*. (Sugita, Y. Ed.). Okayama: Daigaku Kyoiku Shuppan.

Yoshida, S. (1982a). 11-14 Japanese Government's Receipt of Stabilization Program. In MOF (Ed.), *The Financial History of Japan: The Allied Occupation Period, 1945-1952. 20, English Documents (Showa Zaiseishi: Shusen kara Kowa made. 20, Eibun Shiryo)*, MOF Ed. (Vol. 20). Toyo Keizai Shimposha.

Zenkoku Gakko Kyushoku R. (2019). Gakko Kyushoku no Rekishi (History of School Lunch System). *Zenkyuren*. Retrieved from https://www.zenkyuren.jp/lunchs.

Appendix A

Saisho no Demingusho Iinkai Iin (The first Deming Prize Committee)
Source: JUSE. (1997). Soritsu Gojunenshi (50 -Year Chronicle). (p. 35)
Tokyo: JUSE.

Honorary Chairperson: William Edwards Deming
Committee Chairperson: Ichiro Ishikawa, Chairperson, JUSE
Committee Members:
    Hyoe Ouchi, Chairman, Statistics Committee, Prime Minister's Office
    Koroku Wada, Chairman, Japanese Standards Association
    Harunari Inoue, Director General, Industrial Technology Agency
    Jiro Enjoji, Editorial Director, Nihon Keizai Shimbun
    Jiro Yamauchi, Professor, University of Tokyo
    Tatsuo Kawada, Professor, Tokyo Institute of Technology
    Motosaburo Masuyama, Lecturer, University of Tokyo
    Shigeru Mizuno, Associate Professor, Tokyo Institute of Technology
    Eizaburo Nishibori, Counselor, Japan Federation of Science and Technology
    Masao Yukawa, Managing Director, Yawata Steel Co.
    Kaneo Niwa, President, Nishinippon Heavy Industries
    Kenichi Koyanagi, Executive Director, Japan Science and Technology Federation
Chief Secretary:
    Masao Goto, Director, Secretariat Division, Statistics Commission, Prime Minister's Office

Secretary:
> Shin Miura, Manager, Technical Section, Mitsui Chemicals Industries, Inc.
>
> Eizo Watanabe, Manager, Omiya Research Section, Taiheiyo Mining Co.
>
> Asaka Tetsuichi, Associate Professor, University of Tokyo
>
> Kaoru Ishikawa, Associate Professor, University of Tokyo
>
> Masao Kogure, Associate Professor, Tokyo Institute of Technology
>
> Heihachi Sakamoto, Professor, Kobe University
>
> Hiroshi Matsumoto, Telecommunications Research Institute, Ministry of Telecommunications
>
> Masayoshi Ito, Engineer, Japan Management Association
>
> Hidehiko Azuma, Technical Officer, Agency of Industrial Science and Technology
>
> Shoichiro Niki, Counselor, Japan Federation of Science and Technology

Appendix B

Source: JUSE. (1997). Soritsu Gojunenshi (50-Year Chronicle). (p. 37) Tokyo: JUSE.

1. The Deming Prize Committee Rules (established in 1951)
   (Committee establishment and operation)
(1) The Chairman of the Deming Prize Committee shall be the Japan Federation of Science and Technology President.
(2) The Chairperson shall appoint the incoming committee secretaries annually immediately following the Deming Prize presentation ceremony.
(3) The Chairperson shall convene Committee and Executive Committee meetings.
(4) The deliberations of the Committee and Executive Committee shall be decided by majority vote, and in the case of a split vote, the Chairperson shall make the final decision.
(5) The Committee and Executive Committee meetings shall be convened with the attendance of at least a majority of the total number of members in attendance.
(6) The Committee and the Executive Committee may form committees to deliberate on necessary matters or appoint academic experts as temporary members to hear their opinions.
   (Duties of the Committee)
(7) The Deming Prize Committee shall be responsible for implementing the Deming Prize Rules.

(8) The Committee will accept nominations for awards from committee members, as well as from numerous candidates, candidate companies, and business establishments, and review them through the regular procedure.
When an awardee or an awarding organization is selected, the Committee shall announce them and publicly provide the award.
(9) The Executive Committee shall perform necessary tasks related to examinations and investigations as a subordinate body of the Committee.
(10) The Committee shall determine the number and extent of the award each year.
(11) The Committee will determine the supplementary prize for the Deming Prize and the number of the awarded prizes each year.
(12) A subcommittee consisting of the Committee secretaries will review the candidates for the award following the Award Rules.
(13) The Committee shall amend, revise, or repeal the rules of the Awards Committee.
(14) The Committee shall prepare and keep records of the decisions of the Committee and the Executive Committee.
(15) The actual travel expenses may be reimbursed if it becomes necessary to conduct site inspections during the review process.
(16) In principle, the expenses of the Deming Prize Committee shall be paid out of the Prize Fund.

2. Deming Prize Regulations

(1) The Deming Prize was established to commemorate Deming, who visited Japan to give guidance on the industrial application of statistical quality control methods.

(2) The Deming Prize Committee awards the Deming Prize to candidates who
  1) excel in theory and application;
  2) have outstanding achievements in applying statistical quality control methods;
  3) contribute to the results of statistical quality control implementation at the company or business site.
(3) The Deming Prize Fund shall mainly consist of royalties from Dr. Deming's lecture transcripts and other books written by Dr. Deming, as well as donations and other contributions from generous donors.
(4) The Deming Prize shall be awarded once each year. The Deming Prize Committee awards the Deming Prize.
(5) The President of the Union of Japanese Scientists and Engineers (JUSE) shall chair the Deming Prize Committee and appoint the members of the Committee.
(6) The rules of the Deming Award Committee shall be determined separately.
(7) The administration of the Deming Prize and the Deming Prize Committee shall be entrusted to the Secretariat of the JUSE. The JUSE shall supervise the Deming Prize Fund.

Appendix C

Permission for Reproduction from
the Union of Japanese Scientists and Engineers

The following parts of this document have been reproduced with permission obtained from the Union of Japanese Scientists and Engineers on September 7, 2023:

Reproduction Permission Letter

Based on the request dated September 6, 2023, we grant permission for the following reproduction and publication:

<Source of Reproduction>
1. "50-Year History of the Union of Japanese Scientists and Engineers Foundation" p.31 Table 1.8 Schedule of 8-day course
2. "50-Year History of the Union of Japanese Scientists and Engineers Foundation" pp.32-33 Dr. Deming's "Wheel of Quality Control"
3. "50-Year History of the Union of Japanese Scientists and Engineers Foundation" p.35 Table 1.9 Members of the first Deming Prize Committee
4. "50-Year History of the Union of Japanese Scientists and Engineers Foundation" p.36 Table 1.10 Program of the 1st Deming Prize Award Ceremony
5. "50-Year History of the Union of Japanese Scientists and Engineers

Foundation" p.37 Deming Prize Committee Rules (established in 1951)
6. "Quality Control" cover page Quality Control Chart and Editorial Policy (English transcription)
7. Union of Japanese Scientists and Engineers English website "JUSE Unions of Japanese Scientists and Engineers" from the "Winners List" section, the item "The Deming Prize for Individuals, The Deming Distinguished Service Award for Dissemination and Promotion (Overseas)"
https://www.juse.or.jp/upload/files/Deming_prize_EN/list/DP2_DPI_202305.pdf

<Destination of Reproduction>
"Reception and Transformation of Science and Technology: Contribution to Quality Control of Public Health by the Pharmaceutical Industry in Occupied Japan, 1945-1952" by SATO Akiko, Kyoto University of Foreign Studies

Subject to the following conditions:
1. The source (literature name, author name, journal name, issue number, publisher, year of publication) must be indicated.
2. The content must not be altered.

Note
The author translated the above document from Japanese into English.

■ About the Author

SATO Akiko

Akiko Sato is a Faculty of Foreign Studies professor at Kyoto University of Foreign Studies. Her research focuses on public health's social and technological history, quality control, languages, and cultures. She examines the intersection of these fields through interdisciplinary perspectives, with particular emphasis on post-war Japan and international technological transfer.

Science and Technology Acceptance and Transformation
: Contribution to Public Health Quality Control by the Pharmaceutical Industry in Occupied Japan, 1945–1952

First edition, 31 January 2025

■ Author	SATO Akiko	
■ Representative	SATO Mamoru	
■ Publisher	DAIGAKU KYOIKU SHUPPAN Co., Ltd.	
	855-4 Nishiichi Minami-ku Okayama-shi, Okayama	
	700-0953 Japan	
	TEL : 086-244-1268 FAX : 086-246-0294	
■ Printer	Morimoto Printing Co.	
■ DTP	HAYASHI Masako	

© SATO Akiko 2025, Printed in Japan
Omission of a Seal of Approval
We will replace any books with missing or incorrectly bound books.
All rights reserved; no part of this publication may be reproduced or transmitted by any means, electronic, mechanical, photocopying or otherwise, without the prior permission of the publisher.
Please send your comments and suggestions about this publication to the website at right.

ISBN978-4-86692-329-1